WOMEN AT WORK IN MEDIEVAL EUROPE

Madeleine Pelner Cosman

Checkmark Books®
An imprint of Facts On File, Inc.

To one of my favorite modern women at work
my daughter
MARIN COSMAN
lawyer, cantor, friend

Women at Work in Medieval Europe

Checkmark Books
An imprint of Facts On File, Inc.
11 Penn Plaza
New York NY 10001

Library of Congress Cataloging-in-Publication Data
The Library of Congress has cataloged the Facts On File edition as follows:
Cosman, Madeleine Pelner.
Women at work in medieval Europe / by Madeleine Pelner Cosman.
p.   cm.
Includes bibliographical references and index.
ISBN 0-8160-3125-8 (alk. paper) (hc) ISBN 0-8160-4566-6 (pbk)
1. Women—Employment—Europe—History. 2. Women—History—Middle Ages,
500–1500. 3. Social history—Medieval, 500-1500. I. Title.
HD6134.C67 2000
331.4'094'0902—dc21   99-047886

Checkmark Books are available at special discounts when purchased in bulk quantities for
businesses, associations, institutions or sales promotions. Please call our Special Sales
Department in New York at 212/967-8800 or 800/322-8755.

You can find Facts On File on the World Wide Web at http://www.factsonfile.com.

Text design by Evelyn Horovicz
Cover design by Semadar Megged

Printed in the United States of America.

MP FOF 10 9 8 7 6 5 4 3 2 1
(pbk) 10 9 8 7 6 5 4 3 2 1

This book is printed on acid-free paper.

CONTENTS

ACKNOWLEDGMENTS

The Metropolitan Museum of Art in New York initiated this book. As a medical lawyer, I had written about medieval women physicians in medical malpractice legislation and litigation and public health regulations of water, food, and wine. The Metropolitan invited me to emphasize the women and titled one of my annual Met lecture series Medieval Women at Work. I joyously acknowledge that intellectual debt, among others, to my lawyer and professorial colleagues, my medical students, and personal friends.

In my lecturing on medical policy and ethics at seminars at the Universities of Colorado and Virginia I benefited from the Ayn Randian logic of the participants. At the City University of New York I enjoyed the intellectual gifts of the faculty and students of the medical law program and of the Institute for Medieval and Renaissance Studies, which for 28 years I directed.

My late literary agent, Susan Urstadt, brought this book to Facts On File, and Jeanne Fredericks, Susan's able successor, saw this book through production. Senior Editor Mary Kay Linge welcomed it after Caroline Sutton commissioned it, and Cynthia Yazbek guarded it to hard covers.

I gratefully acknowledge the expertise of librarians, curators, and directors of the libraries and museums whose documents I used in London, Oxford, Cambridge, Rome, Venice, Vienna, and Prague. In New York, I enjoyed the graciousness of the Morgan Library, New York Academy of Medicine, New York Botanical Gardens, Jewish Theological Seminary, Columbia University, Benjamin Cardozo School of Law, and the Frick Museum. Lastly, I celebrate the Geisel Library of the University of California–San Diego and the Library of the United States Supreme Court.

INTRODUCTION

Medieval women worked in professions and crafts that we often think were closed to them before the modern era. Professionally successful medieval women writers and artists, physicians and surgeons, political and church leaders, commercial bakers, fabric weavers, and mineral miners thrived in their crafts, earning good salaries and wages, meriting honor and reputation, and coexisting (usually benevolently, sometimes antagonistically) with medieval men.

Just as women thrived in the world of labor, other women were notorious in the underworld as prostitutes, thieves, and felons. Records of the professional activity of medieval women in western Europe between the 10th and 15th centuries enable modern people to appreciate the sexual balance in medieval society and the important history of women at work. The medieval world was not entirely dominated by men. Medieval splendor was not created by men alone.

Medieval data is easy to misinterpret because what remains has been selectively preserved, and some scholars inadvertently or intentionally distort the historical record. Virulently antifeminist treatises describing the viciousness or helplessness or uselessness of women often are interpreted as reflecting medieval women's actual lives. But these texts were primarily composed by clerics to promote celibacy and sexual continence among the clergy. Clerical chastisement of women from the pulpits and in literature was expedient to enable churchmen to disdain what they should not love and could not have.

WOMEN AT WORK IN MEDIEVAL EUROPE

Farm women worked as partners with their husbands. Women laboring for others customarily were paid equal wages as men for the same work. Women inheriting land from their parents or as widows from their husbands worked land for themselves or hired local or itinerant men or women laborers. Manor account books, tax rolls, and law court records are treasure-troves of data for woman's life on the land. In 14th-century England, peasants' heredity of land and family name were so united that a man marrying a landed peasant often adopted her maiden name or her late husband's name. In the Oxfordshire village of Cuxham, Gilbert Bourdoun married widow Sarah le Wyte and became Gilbert le Wyte. Christine de Pizan, in her instruction book for women, The Book of the Three Virtues, addressed women farmers as the ones "by whose labor the world gains its sustenance and nourishment," who have neither leisure nor luxury to serve God through church-going, fasting, and prayer meetings in town. But they must serve God and themselves through honest dealings with other farmers and villagers and through ethical payments in labor or goods. Women legally owing the overlord wheat are to pay with grain grown on the land, not mixing in cheap oats. If owing payments in livestock, they are not to hide the good ewes and best rams at their neighbors' in order to pay with inferior animals. Nor should they give dishonest accountings of carts, property, or poultry. Women should admonish their husbands to equally honest exchanges of value for value.

Opposite: Physicians treat a dying man as his family gathers in prayer. Female doctors, well-trained in the healing arts, were licensed to practice throughout medieval Europe. A man scrutinizes the patient's urine while two women attend at his bed. A young man entering the room is the heir to the fortune he counts in the margin below, the treasure chest open. Books of hours, the personal prayerbooks for the wealthy, often depict such secular events as death with humor, cynicism, and social commentary. Here the richly-robed, eager young heir surveys his wealth before his benefactor dies.

In medieval contracts, marriage documents, wills, bills of sale, law court opinions, medical texts and records, commercial papers, and works of art we find an altogether different picture of medieval women's professional activities, legal status, cultural achievements, and interactions with men.

Law documents are particularly revealing. Usually they articulate several opposing ideas about the same subject. Medieval medical malpractice litigation chronicles cases of women surgeons sued for incompetence. The records preserve diametrically opposed interpretations of physician, patient, and medical establishment through the testimony of expert witnesses and the opinions of the citizens who judged innocence or guilt. Legislation and litigation documents, free of the prejudices of one individual author or a single political agenda, allow the wonderful possibility of understanding the truth about medieval women. At least, they offer an impressive contrast to misogynistic depictions of women in medieval literature and art.

Medieval laws recognized the *femme sole* (an Old French phrase for "woman alone") who was an independent businesswoman or craftswoman, responsible by law for her own professional practice, purchases, profits, and business debts. The term was not simply equivalent to *spinster:* a married woman could be designated a *femme sole* for legally protecting her business assets against financial incursions of greedy relatives or her husband.

Modern family names preserve the heritage of medieval women at work. Matronymics are family names traced through the mother's lineage and profession. The family name *Baxter* derives from a medieval female professional baker. Progeny of a male bread and cake maker use the name Baker. *Webster* comes from a woman ancestor in the cloth trade. A male cloth maker's descendant is named Weaver or Webber. *Brewster* is a family name descending from a woman beer or ale maker; her male colleague was a Brewer. The family name *Lavender* originates with a woman launderer or fabric handler. A man in that textile craft passed down the name Laver.

Studying women at work reveals qualities shared by the noble and commoner, the rich and poor, the educated and illiterate, the young and old, the Christian and Jew. Rather than emphasizing a few specific medieval women, legal documents democratize a past reality. The illustrious in medicine, literature, brewery, and mining coexist with ordinary women and men colleagues. In medieval legal and business records, the notorious commingle with the obscure.

Both men and women will appreciate *Women at Work in Medieval Europe*'s emphasis on working women and their remarkable achievements in the arts and sciences. People accustomed to thinking that medieval life was circumscribed by church restrictions and entirely dominated by men will be startled at depictions of women's power in professions and crafts, as well as by medieval men's honoring women's work. Modern enthusiasts marvel at the concept of naming children by the professions of their mother: John Baxter, Julienne Brewster, Neil Webster, names demonstrating today the venerable, durable heritage of medieval working women. Modern readers exult in learning about women's professional guilds which in music and in such lucrative fabric trades as France's silk weaving industry vigorously celebrated women's excellence.

The glories of the medieval world are not for medievalists alone. This book incorporates original documents which I hope will inform your museum visits, castle treks in Europe, marriage (or divorce) ceremonies, contracts for buying a house, or exquisite dinners with fine wines. These modern events preserve medieval customs. *Women at Work in Medieval Europe* is a treasury for people passionate about the Middle Ages, who respect works of excellence created by both men and women.

Consider the hidden heritage of women professional writers, poets, and artists. Castelloza and Countess de Dia, 12th-century women troubadours, Marie de France, a writer of exquisite *lais,* Marguerite de Navarre, the creator of the *Heptameron,* and other professional writers achieved renown in their time and place, also affecting other peoples and nations. Marie de France influenced later writers in England, France, and Germany. Christine de Pizan was a notable international cultural force who affected the thought and behavior of both women and men in France, Portugal, and England.

Five of Christine de Pizan's 20 books are dedicated specifically to women's education and encouragement. She adressed her instruction book on chivalry and armor to knights at arms. William Caxton, England's earliest printer and publisher, translated one of Christine de Pizan's books rolling it from his press soon after he published the Bible. Caxton called Christine "the mirror and mistress of intelligence." The poet Eustache Deschamps lauded her learning, and Martin le Franc insisted that Christine de Pizan equaled Cicero for eloquence and Cato for wisdom.

Consider the excellence of medieval women physicians, surgeons, and pharmacists. Legislation against medical malpractice, and litigation the laws promoted, yield fascinating demonstrations of the power and perils of educated, licensed women physicians and surgeons from the 12th through the 15th centuries. Close analysis of medical laws within their linguistic contexts demonstrates that the customary assumption that medieval women physicians were regarded as merely "old wives" and uneducated charlatans is a ludicrous misinterpretation of bona fide laws prohibiting women practitioners from abusing their professional status. Those same documents uniformly prohibit *men* physicians and surgeons from malpractice. The purpose of the legislation and subsequent court

Pages xii–xiii: Parades and public processions served politics as well as practical safe transport from place to place. Likewise, a "progress" was a ceremonial journey from one castle to another to examine landholdings, to provide personal and legal oversight, and to reaffirm political control. Here at an international church conference in Constance, Germany, the empress and emperor process with visiting royalty, courtiers, and clergymen dignitaries. Men's and women's headdresses signified rank as well as asserted the latest fashion and the wealth to buy it. Accompanying the crowned women attended by men servants and courtiers, lower left, are gentlewomen, lower right, wearing fashionable fabric turbans called chaperones *with extravagantly long, decorative cloth tails called* liripipes, *pendent down the back or swung over the shoulder, ornamented with bells, fringes, or semiprecious stones.*

WOMEN AT WORK IN MEDIEVAL EUROPE
xii

cases is not condemnation of women but celebration of vigorous medical standards in cities such as London, Paris, Ferrara, Rome, and Florence whose dedicated laws protected four constituencies: patient, practitioner, professional guild, and citizenry.

Glimpses into the lives and works of typical practitioners can be got from these medico-legal archives and commercial documents. Art historians may argue about whether an androgynously costumed creature on a painted battlefield treating wounded soldiers is male or female, and then from modern social prejudices label the putative male a doctor and the female a nurse. But payment receipts for medical war services sometimes distinguish sex unequivocally, showing that salaries and stipends were paid both to male surgeons and to female surgeons, such as Dr. Barbara of Wissenkirchen, a battlefield trauma surgeon in 14th-century Germany.

Dr. Jacqueline Felicia of Paris was accused of medical malpractice in 1322. Over half a millennium later, we can still read the court testimony of her grateful men and women patients attesting to her reputation and her cures. Hildegard of Bingen, poet, mystic, abbess, and physician, specialized in treating epilepsy. Her encyclopedic medical texts describe disease vectors in transmission of communicable diseases. She humanely suggested mechanical painkillers when botanical and mineral analgesics, soporifics, and anesthetics were unavailable or ineffectual. She also advocated what modern readers can choose to interpret as silly lapidary superstition or as early biofeedback techniques, such as using solace stones, semiprecious gems smoothed and polished to sensual texture, held in the hand and rubbed to mitigate the pain of childbirth, and flattened oval agate stones to be held in the cheek to forestall hunger pangs for dieters.

Consider also the women leaders and rulers of manors and monasteries. Lady bosses directing secular and ecclesiastical enterprises were common. In 1409, Christine de Pizan wrote a notable instruction and etiquette book for such powerful women. A typical day in the life of a lady boss vested with enormous authority as princess, baroness, or lady, demonstrates the excruciating activities and ceremonies of leadership.

Exercising authority so that her power was acknowledged and reaffirmed, the lady boss usually was government leader or counselor, paymaster, and supervisor of the household. A household sometimes was the size of a town with farms, bake houses, cloth weaving factories, castles, forests, rental properties, churches, and priories. All needed planning, staffing, directing, coordinating, budgeting, and other classical functions of organization a chief executive exercises.

Far from being homebound, women leaders participated in the rigors of riding to crusade, the arduous, ceremonial voyages called "progresses" to visit landholdings, the political travels to new acquisitions got by diplomacy or war, the visits to markets, fairs, and banking houses, and the defense of their possession by sword and cross-bow. Their energy is exemplified by the superbly vigorous (also literary and loquacious) 15th-century Englishwoman Margaret Paston, whose letters to her family (her husband and son at court) and to statesmen demonstrate magnificently the practices of women leaders. For example, while defending her castle under siege, she sent a shopping list to her husband at court in London requesting battle-axes and armaments plus silks and woolen cloth for their children's winter clothing.

Ecclesiastical women rulers, such as the abbesses Hilda of Whitby, Hersende of Fontevrault, and Héloïse of Paraclete, exemplify women administrators guiding and guarding both the daily life and the immortal souls of their co-religious.

By intention I have selected from vast European archives exemplary women practitioners because documents of their exploits met my criteria for authenticity, and for demonstrating medieval woman's range of professional activity. Though I strove to include typical achievements of medieval European working women, I certainly could not ignore spectacular examples, such as the professional writer Christine de Pizan.

This book offers the grand tour of medieval European women's work. It sets an intellectual context into which special investigations of a particular nation's professional women fit. No history dares claim absolute truth. Nevertheless, medieval legal documents of women at work, with their necessarily adversarial attempts to distinguish the true from false, the right from wrong, the real from fantasy, permit bright glimpses into medieval magnificence.

WOMEN WRITERS
AND POETS

$\mathcal{S}$ome medieval women writers, sensitive to psychological nuances, delightfully depicted feelings and emotions. So did some medieval men writers. Some medieval women artists, like their male contemporaries, wrote exquisitely of human love and suffering. Other women writers dedicated themselves to moral instruction, uplifting the spirit towards high ideals or to God. Some women wrote love poems, dramas, romances, satires, courtly etiquette books, imaginary voyages, and political panegyrics. Some women writers, such as Christine de Pizan, published state histories, royal biographies, political treatises, translations from the classics, literary diatribes, and instruction books on chivalry and warfare. Some women writers staunchly defended the reputation of womanhood. Some women wrote antifeminist, woman-damning humorous tales. Some women wrote bawdy, sexually titillating, rude, crude, lewd tales.

Among the delights of reading medieval women writers is the variety of their subjects and literary types. A supremely talented artist such as Christine de Pizan equaled any male colleague in skill and popularity. A few more banal literary women wrote works as interesting or dull as poetry and prose by their mediocre men colleagues. The best medieval women writers achieved the medieval literary ideal of *docere et delectare,* instructing while pleasing and delighting while informing.

Opposite: With her pet dog observing, Christine de Pizan, the prolific 15th-century professional author, writes in her study, seated on a high-backed chair and working at a sloping desk. Natural light streams in through her window. Her hat is on and her pen in hand. A box with pen nibs and ink is open beside her book. Christine was said to be an excellent calligrapher and may have been her own scribe for some manuscripts among her 20 published books.

Medieval women writers merit scrupulous critical attention and enthusiastic modern acclaim. Exemplifying the range of medieval European women authors are four women who wielded the pen for pleasure and for profit. Each earned money and reputation by the vigor of her ideas and the excellence of her craft.

The Countess de Dia was a 12th-century woman troubadour. One of the best of a group of nearly 20 intelligent, literate, artistically productive women writing poetry in Occitania, the south of France, she wrote in the so-called *lange d'oc,* or Provençal.

The second notable woman writer was Marie de France, whose poetic *lais* and fables charmingly, astutely depict courtly love's most extravagant imaginings, complete with magic, marvels, and werewolves. Marie also wrote hilarious, erotic, coarse tales of ingenious wives cuckolding their husbands while rejoicing in their own wit and their power over men.

Christine de Pizan superbly composed treatises, histories, allegories, letters, dream visions, instruction books, love songs, political essays, and five major books dedicated specifically to women, including the women's utopia, *The City of Ladies.* Christine supported herself, her three children, her mother, and miscellaneous relatives by her writing. Significant noble patrons of 15th-century France commissioned her work. Christine de Pizan was not only popular in her time and place but was appreciated as an international intellectual figure, praised for excellence and learning. William Caxton, England's first printer, presented Christine de Pizan's work among the first volumes he printed in English. First Caxton published the Bible. Next he translated Christine de Pizan.

A fourth formidable female writer was Marguerite de Navarre, duchess of Alençon and queen of Navarre, whose early dramas and poems were highly moral, moralistic, and sententious. However, just as

WOMEN WRITERS AND POETS

3

Marguerite de Navarre merits comparison to her Renaissance contemporary, the philosopher Montaigne, equally Marguerite indulged her wit in humorous, sexy, scatological stories, like her compatriot Rabelais. Marguerite de Navarre's *Heptameron,* meant in part to imitate Boccaccio's *Decameron,* consists of 72 tales told by 10 *devisants* or storytellers who comment philosophically and realistically after each tale. An influential literary and cultural force, she drew to her court thinkers and artists who credited their achievements to her encouragement and her money.

Countess de Dia, Marie de France, Christine de Pizan, and Marguerite de Navarre all were wellborn, educated members of an intellectual aristocracy they entered by birth, marriage, or professional association with courts of the nobility. Do these four women sing with women's voices? Do they and their contemporaries write about women's subjects? Or with women's styles?

TROUBADOURS

The Countess de Dia, one of the finest of the *trobaritz* (women troubadours), probably did not have to sing for her supper. She sang to solace her pain. Or so the conventions of courtly love required. In 12th-century Occitania, troubadour lyrics in Provençal expressed a mannered passion. The "I" who sings of love is not necessarily telling social truth so much as demonstrating expertise in popular artistic style.

Troubadour songs of courtly love conventionally depict a male lover praising with exquisite exaggeration a highborn, imperious lady who stoops to return his affection only if he prostrates himself humbly and serves her faithfully. Likewise, the female troubadour adulates her beloved, but rarely so abjectly.

Courtly love, as defined in such 12th-century texts as Andreas Capellanus's *Art of Courtly Love,* is an inborn suffering derived from the sight of and contemplation upon the beloved. Love inspires the lover to wondrous feats of arms or of art. Conversely, love confuses and distracts, causing forgetfulness of work, clothing, and wit itself. Death is preferable to unanswered affection.

Love is service to the beloved. Courtly love places the lover in relationship to the beloved as the suppliant vassal before a feudal overlord, or as the supplicating believer begging mercy of God.

Literary love worship doubtlessly was influenced by earlier literary traditions Latin, Christian, and Arabic, but patronage also contributed. Troubadours worked for courts inhabited by or directed by strong, intelligent, appreciative women. Poetry flourished in the manors and castles of such women art patrons as Eleanor of Aquitaine, her daughter Marie of Champagne, and in courts of lesser-known patronesses such as Ermengarda of Narbonne. Professional court entertainers, men and women troubadours were paid to praise and pleased by praising. The troubadour's beloved oftentimes was both the patron and the praised. Significantly, many a troubadour laments forgetfulness in payment or stinginess, complaining in poetry to an empty purse. Though such complaints also are literary conventions, nevertheless they suggest that professional considerations dictated troubadour lyrics as much as private passion.

Literary courtly love, or *fin amor,* almost invariably is an adulterous affair. The noble lover is another person's spouse. Secrecy is essential to protect the lovers and their lives. Conventional characters people these complex, preciously-wrought poems. The cuckolded spouse is depicted as jealous, actually referred to as the envious one, the *gelos,* whom the lovers must deceive without being caught by the *lozengiers,* the court scandalmongers.

Countess de Dia writes: "Fin amor, fine joy brings me great happiness, which makes me sing more gaily. It doesn't bother me a bit that those sneaky *lozengiers* are out to harm me. Their evil talk doesn't dismay me. Their chatter makes me twice as exuberant."

In troubadour lyrics the lover generally addresses the beloved through trusted intermediaries, sometimes friends, servants, or pets such as a faithful dog carrying messages between the furtive lovers. Prudence requires that if the love note is intercepted it cannot definitively identify the sender or reveal the receiver. The lover is addressed by a code name, a *senjal.* Secrecy, utilitarian in literary or actual illicit affairs, elegantly endures.

Love's pain, though personally distressing, is artistic stimulus. As Countess de Dia's compatriot, the woman troubadour Castelloza, writes: "God knows I should have had my fill of song. The more I sing the worse I fare in love." And again: "Friend, if you had shown consideration, humility, and humanity, I would have loved you without hesitation. But you are mean, sly, and villainous. Still I compose this song to spread your praises far and wide for I can't bear to let your name go unsung."

Women troubadours speak directly, with few euphemisms, of love, the art of loving, and their lovers. Trobaritz poems scintillate with candor—

or seem to. It is an open question how far these love lyrics are autobiography and how far well-crafted literature.

Strong-minded and strong-willed in their poetry, lady troubadours insist upon their prerogative to express love. Countess de Dia says, "The lady who understands valor should dare to love a worthy knight face to face." The countess fervently declares: "How I wish just once I could caress that knight with my bare arms, in ecstasy lean his head against my breast. Oh handsome friend, if only I could lie beside you for an hour and embrace you lovingly. I would give anything to have you in my husband's place."

Art requires the troubadour Castelloza to tell nasty truths, such as her lover's infidelity. Her poetry also depicts a romantic ideal of love at first sight. "Since first I saw you I have been at your command. If it would do me any good, I would remind you, singing, that I stole your glove, trembling. When a lady's mind is set on love she ought to court the man." In yet another poem Castelloza relates: "I want to prove that courting brings me great relief when I court the man who brought me grief."

Castelloza and Countess de Dia were professional poets who expected cold cash for their passionate lines in addition to appreciation by readers or hearers. Castelloza's family and her husband gained glory from her pain.

While some medieval women poets may have written cool, limpid lines to quell hot ardor in their breasts, few learned, intelligent women, then or now, preserve their heart-longings in songs with such contrived verse forms, complicated rhyme schemes, formulaic phrases, strict rhythmic patterns, word plays, and the artistic trappings of troubadour preciosity. Women troubadours, like such great men poets as Bernart de Ventadorn, Bertrand de Born, and Gaucelme Faidit, celebrated strict artistic restraints.

Troubadours praised for profit. The woman troubadour Isabella exchanges amorous barbs in a *tenson,* a poetic debate, with the troubadour Elias Cairel. Isabella accuses him of turning his love songs from her to another. He replies, "Lady Isabella, if in those days I sang your praises it was not out of love, but for profit. Likewise any paid poet (*joglar*) sings a lady's fame."

Lady poets also sang ladies' fame. The *trobaritz* Aralais dedicates a poem to the patroness Ermengarda. The woman troubadour Bieiras writes passionate praise of a woman known only as Marìa. If such poems are autobiographical, then Bieiras may have loved Marìa as Sappho loved the young ladies of Lesbos. Homosexual or heterosexual, the mannered passion of troubadour poems created splendid art.

Women troubadours produced bravura works, ingeniously using traditional components in new ways. Like their male contemporaries, masterly women poets used tradition for individualistic purposes, inserting personal commentary and social observations within poetic conventions. An amusing instance is the poem in which two sisters request advice from the Lady Carenza. "Shall I marry? Or shall I stay unwed? Independence would please me. Making babies doesn't seem appealing. And it's too anguishing to be a wife. Though I would enjoy having a husband, making babies is a huge penitence. Your breasts hang way down. It is just too anguishing to be a wife."

Though troubadour lyrics originally were written as songs, relatively few musical settings have survived the passing of the centuries. Countess de Dia wrote both lyric and melody for a magnificent lament upon an inconstant lover. "I must sing of things I would rather keep silent. With him my mercy and fine manners are in vain. My beauty, my virtue, and my intelligence count for nought. He has tricked me and cheated me. My lover is gone."

MARIE DE FRANCE

Other 12th-century writers utilized courtly love themes in conjunction with characters from Arthurian romance, creating poems and prose for a popular audience which included both the educated and the untutored. Though skillfully wrought works of art, these writings are more powerful in their story than refined in their style. Great traditional stories newly fashioned pleased the audience which paid men and women writers to create these entertainments.

Twelfth-century poet Marie de France was a grand storyteller whose works for an English court superbly preserve medieval noble interest in magic, mysticism, marvels, manners, ceremonies, and brutal cruelty. Her Arthurian tales compare favorably with the romances of Chrétien de Troyes. A deft story-spinner, Marie also was a humorist whose ribaldry ranks with the finest medieval sexual humor. Her fabliaux depict women exulting in their sexuality, using anatomy as well as language and wit to control their fates.

Marie de France was famous also for her *lais,* those poetic short tales once meant to be sung or chanted. Today she is best-known for her delightful fables whose animal characters depict the moral foibles, follies, and failures of men and women.

Her writings sometimes are judged antifeminist for depicting cunning, wily women. Some of her books are dedicated to men—her *lais* to an unnamed king, and her fables and fabliaux to a Count William—and she revels in portraying women and words. Word themes dominate Marie de France's work: women and promises, women and rash pledges, women plighting troths, women's language being other than what it seems, women's word taboos, women's word formulae bringing luck or compelling disaster. Are Marie de France's tales necessarily anti-woman? Briefly let us consider two *lais* and two fabliaux.

A beautiful, noble, viper-tongued woman slandered her neighbor, who had just given birth to twin sons. The slanderer insisted that any woman who bore two children simultaneously was an adulterer who made each child by a different father.

Her nasty, defamatory word echoed in her own womb. She herself soon bore twin daughters. Recognizing that an accusation of adultery would be leveled against her, the new mother insisted upon killing one daughter. Her attendant gentlewomen refused to carry out this infanticide. But her confidante took one unwanted babe, placing her safely with rich blankets and jewelry in an ash tree across from a convent.

The nuns, retrieving the rich and beautiful babe, raised her as their own. Once grown, the foundling loved a splendid knight. Though they did not marry, they lived in bliss.

One day the nobleman's countrymen demanded that he marry a woman to produce heirs for his realm. His counselors chose his wife for him. She was the twin sister of his beloved.

Faithful Fresne, she who had been found in the ash tree, decorated his unwilling bed with the beautiful blankets which were her only inheritance. Though now betrayed, she loved him unconditionally.

The mother of the bride, coming to inspect the nuptial bed, recognized the fateful fabrics, and Fresne, her long-lost daughter. After tearful recognitions and forgiveness, the young lord and Fresne, his mistress, married. A new husband was found for the twin sister. Each couple wedded and bedded happily thereafter.

The sharp-tongued woman's word controlled her life. Rashly she had said what she should not. Yet she could not take back words once uttered.

She was obliged to atone for them, expiate them in actions within her own life.

Language's power and the potency of word prompt Marie's women characters to other forms of betrayal than infanticide. In another *lai,* a woman's word is pitted against love's constancy and a man's promises.

A fine courtly couple loved one another dearly. But the wife was perplexed by the husband's absence several nights per week. He refused to reveal the reason for it. After promising never to tell his secret, she begged him to tell her how and where he spent his time. He reluctantly revealed that, though a trusted courtier of the king, by night he became a werewolf.

So long as he had access to his clothing, he could assure his transformation back to his handsome human body. Clothing lost, he would be doomed to wander forever in wolf's skin.

The once-loving wife, hearing the secret unwillingly shared, suddenly was revolted by living with a sometime werewolf. Enlisting the help of the man who loved her, she hid the werewolf's clothes, condemning him to wolf life. The wife married her lover.

The disconsolate wolf now became the king's faithful animal companion. Though as docile and gallant a wolf as he had been a courtier, the entrapped werewolf one day attacked the wife's lover, nearly killing him at court.

The king recognized that his intelligent animal was using the only language allowed him, namely snarls, growls, bites, and ripping flesh. The king questioned, then threatened, the werewolf's wife. In tearful confession she revealed her treachery.

Discreetly left alone in a room with his clothing, the werewolf's transmuted himself from beast to man. He regained his rightful position at court. His despicable wife and her lover were banished from the kingdom forever.

Marie de France's werewolf is the most elegantly refined beast of blood ever to stalk a midnight forest. He is neither grotesque nor Draculesque. Though he has sworn never to reveal his secret self, he breaks his pledge. Though his wife has given her word never to divulge his secret, she nefariously tells her lover. In Marie's work, as in much medieval literature, once the sanctity of the word is broken, once the power of the word is loose, nothing can control it.

Noble wily women manipulate word in Marie's courtly *lais.* Peasant women also talk their way out of compromising situations in Marie's fabliaux. As with the *lais,* the fabliaux are derived from traditional liter-

Opposite: A high-breasted, tightly-gowned young woman wearing a fashionable reticulated headdress entertains an older, balding, bearded lover whose hand rests suggestively in his front pocket of his tunic. Either he touches his anatomy or fingers his money. He wears a fashionable, fur-trimmed short tunic with pointed poulaine slippers, though his hat, removed at his side, is more rustic and practical than stylish. The couple having traveled by horseback from the castle or town in the background, their horse scratches its back on the tree to which it is tethered. The man may represent the typical senex amans, *the foolish old man in love, a stock character in medieval art, humor, fiction, and especially the* fabliaux. *The woman's exuberant sexuality plus the old man's folly leads to an inevitable love triangle. If they marry, she takes a young lover to cuckold her husband. If the young woman has the old man as secret lover, or if she is a professional prostitute, she pleases him whether or not he pleases her and takes personal sexual satisfaction with another man.*

ary and folk themes which Marie magnificently transforms. Here are two of Marie de France's tales of women and their paramours.

An old peasant returning home looked through his house-door into his bedroom. There he saw his own young wife disporting herself on their bed with a strange man.

"Alas," he later cried to his wife, "what have I seen? Another man was on my bed holding you tight in his embrace." The wife, enraged, said, "This is your old foolishness. You hold a lie for the truth."

"I see," he said, "and I must believe." She replied, "You are crazy if you believe that whatever you see is true." She takes him by the hand, leads him to a barrel filled with water, makes him look into the barrel, and asks what he sees. He notes his own reflection.

"Are you in that barrel? It seems that you are in the water in the barrel wearing all your clothes. You see with your own eyes that you are in there. But you are not there. You only seem to be there. You should not have faith in what you see. Appearances lie."

"I repent," says the elderly peasant. "Everyone had better believe that what his wife says is truer than what he sees with his poor eyes. Eyes often deceive by appearances."

Marie's final comment is: "Intellect and trickery are more worthy and more helpful than goods or heritage."

Another peasant saw his wife going towards the woods with her lover. He went home completely furious. Upon her returning home he reviled and scolded her. He revealed he had seen her with her seducer in shame and dishonor.

"Sire," she said, "for the love of God tell me the truth. Did you see a man accompanying me?"

"I saw him!" he replied.

Dramatically wringing her hands, she answered: "Alas, I am dead! I shall die tomorrow. Perhaps I die today. It happened thus to my mother and to my grandmother. A little before their deaths, a young man was seen leading them away when no one was actually with them. Now I know my end is near."

The peasant cried for mercy. "Let it be, my darling. Do not leave me. All that I saw was a lie."

"No," she answered, "I dare not remain longer. I am a goner. But if you will swear upon your oath that you never saw a man with me and will never speak a word about it, I will stay." Together they went to a monastery where he there swore what she asked.

Marie's moral to this tale: "Women know well how to deceive. Women are untrustworthy schemers who know more tricks than the Devil."

Are Marie de France's tales antifeminist? Women of Marie's fabliaux are similar to Geoffrey Chaucer's lusty, gutsy, wives of aged, sexually senescent men in tales such as the "Miller's Tale" and the "Reeve's Tale" in the *Canterbury Tales*. Marie de France's women, like Chaucer's, talk themselves into benefits while they talk themselves out of danger. They delight in deceit. Gleefully they manipulate word by wit. They triumph over their husbands' selfish follies. Women's exultant sexuality is well paired with ingenuity to indulge it.

Fabliaux women, especially those in tales written by women, are an alphabetical catalogue of liveliness: they are able, ardent, audacious, amorous, baiting, bored beauties, carnally curious, cuckolding coquettes. Fabliaux women are daring in their duping of doddering husbands, engagingly effervescent in feisty philandering. In Marie de France's fabliaux, women are not mean nor vulgar nor vicious. Fabliaux women are enthusiasts. They are physically energetic and linguistically nimble.

Marie de France beautifully uses the folklore *märchen,* the old theme of the foolish old man in love who inevitably invites his own cuckolding.

This traditional *senex amans* unwittingly initiates the adulterous triangle by jealously guarding his lively young wife, and tempting her to steal her freedom from his cruel restrictions. I suspect that many anonymous fabliaux were written by women, just as outrageously humorous and blasphemous marginalia of manuscripts may have been illuminated by bold women artists unafraid to caricature the sacred.

CHRISTINE DE PIZAN

A medieval woman professional writer who dexterously balanced the politics of sex with excellence of craft is Christine de Pizan, a startlingly effective apologist for intelligent, creative, productive women. Among her 20 major works, five are devoted to women's history or women's instruction. Elegant, practical, rigorous argument Christine paired with clever literary devices. An international cultural figure, Christine affected both the entertainments and the lives of women in several countries. Christine's works were translated from French to English and Portuguese.

Counting among her noble patrons the rich and powerful Burgundian bibliophiles, Christine supported herself and family entirely by proceeds of her pen. In addition to being a superb composer of poetry and prose, she apparently also was a talented scribe-copyist who produced some of her own beautifully calligraphed manuscripts. She may have illustrated and illuminated some of those works. Studious, scholarly, passionate, and clever, Christine de Pizan transformed personal misfortune into opportunity, expertly making a virtue of necessity.

From Italy, Christine de Pizan arrived in Paris with her illustrious father, the court physician to King Charles V. Growing up at the royal court, she married, at 15, Étienne du Castelle, the king's secretary and a prominent member of his chancery, with whom she lived in an idyllic marriage of mutual respect for 10 years. Her husband, abroad on a diplomatic mission, died suddenly during an epidemic. Christine, aged 25, was left with three children, an aging mother, and precarious finances. Talent and intellect might have inspired her writings, but necessity drove her to work.

Intermittently forced to law court to obtain her widow's legacy, and reduced to selling furnishings from her castle, she soon established so fine a reputation as a writer that she was commissioned to write official royal biographies, works on statecraft, warfare, manners, morals, and love.

In an era appreciating eloquence and stylistic elegance, Christine's versatility was matched by her verbal virtuosity. Her works are important first for their notable substance and style. Her writings form an intriguing portrait of France in the year 1400. No other known medieval woman writer produced so large a volume of significant works.

England in the 1400s adored Christine as avidly as did France. Caxton translated Christine's *Moral Proverbs* as one of the first books to roll from his Westminster press in London. For at least 100 years after her death, Christine de Pizan's instruction book for women, published in England as *The Book of the Three Virtues,* was many times reprinted. It is a book of etiquette and statecraft for women in power in politics, in professions, and in trade.

William Caxton, England's first printer, called Christine de Pizan the "mirror and mistress of intelligence." The French poet Eustache Deschamps lauded her as "handmaid of learning," commending her valiant conduct of her occupation as a professional writer. Deschamps called himself her disciple and admirer. A visitor to Paris in 1407, describing the intellectual life of the city with delightful hyperbole, said that Paris possessed 60,000 scholars, professionals, musicians, and writers, prominent among whom is Damoselle Christine de Pizan. Martin le Franc, in his 15th-century poem "The Champion of Women," maintained that many French women "put men to shame both in fields and cities, and particularly Christine, the equal of Cicero for eloquence and Cato for wisdom."

Christine de Pizan's prodigious production merits celebration. During the seven years between 1399 and 1406 she wrote 20 major works. These are distinguished by notable ideas, variety of literary type, and sane insistence upon women's potential for excellence.

She wrote forceful letters defending women against the misogynist Jean de Meun's condemnation in his popular *Romance of the Rose.* Christine elegantly, cogently argues woman's cause. In historiography Philip, Duke of Burgundy, commissioned Christine de Pizan to write the life history of his brother King Charles V. With distinction, against such adversities as uncooperative people refusing to tell her what they knew, she created a nationalistic panegyric that is also a treasury of fact, anecdote, and dramatic vignette.

Her "Vision of Christine," though a conventional medieval dream vision, complete with personified virtues, vices, magic, and marvels, is also autobiography. She deplores her evil fortune but reaffirms both God's will and her own talents. Lamenting her husband's early death, she recognizes that his death tested her patience. Equally, it allowed her freedom from household chores which otherwise might have prevented her studying and writing.

Christine's treatise on warfare is an analysis of chivalry and manners, popularizing a classical work on warfare by Vegetius. England's King Henry VII thought the book crucial for every "gentleman born to arms and all manner men of war." The king commissioned Caxton to translate and print Christine's volume as the *Book of Feats of Arms and Chivalry.*

Before glimpsing the charm, intelligence, and power of three of Christine's important books, it is helpful to observe a *caveat lector,* a "reader beware" sign. Christine, daughter of her culture, utilized literary techniques that are currently out of fashion. She used stylistic tricks popular when women's tall hats called hennins were as fashionable as flamboyant roast peacock for dinner. But millinery, feasting, and literature have changed during the nearly six centuries since she wrote. Her allegories seem peculiar or forbidding today. Like fine wine tasters, modern readers must train their palates to discern the exquisite tastes of old vintages. Literary and linguistic devices such as allegory now are not fashionable. Yet allegory is not entirely out of our daily language.

Allegory presents abstract ideas as persons or literary characters. Even modern readers unaccustomed to visualizing Anger or Learning as people can acquire a taste for it. Intelligent medieval people easily could envision Wrath as a fiery, frazzle-haired, vicious, knife-wielding woman. Knowledge was a tall, imperious, scholarly lady, faithful to those who faithfully, painfully pursue her, and willing to go with every man wherever he must wander and be his guide.

Christine's passion for allegory is nicely exemplified in her poem with the unpromising title "The Road of Long Studies." Like other medieval dream visions, such as the Gawain poet's *Pearl* and Dante's *Divine Comedy,* Christine's allegory begins with her falling asleep and later writing her testimony of what she saw in the otherworld.

Grieving alone in her study, remembering her beloved husband, Christine as speaker consoles herself by reading Boethius. Moved by his *Consolation of Philosophy,* she continues reading till well past midnight, when she falls asleep. Suddenly in her dream the Cumaean Sibyl appears to Christine and takes her on a world tour of glorious places she has been studying in her long, scholarly reading. Just as Virgil guided Dante

through the other world, Sibylla directs Christine through Byzantium, Africa, and Asia. In each exotic place Christine is tempted by delicate silk fabrics and aromatic spices.

Christine proceeds through this journey undaunted by vast distances. She catapults right into outer space. Not by rocket but by a ladder called *Speculation*, Christine climbs out from the bounds of the globe to see it as a small ball amidst the grand universe of planets, stars, and comets.

Dazzled by the view, and warm from climbing towards the sun, Christine shouts her worry that the frail ladder will not hold her weight. Sibylla answers, "For God's sake trust me! Fear not. You won't melt."

Christine, the court physician's daughter, notes the heavenly persons representing astrological houses, the Zodiac signs controlling the destinies of all beings. Sharing this firmament are four gorgeous queens, women governors of Earthworld, namely Nobility, Wisdom, Wealth, and

Opposite: One of the Seven Virtues, Temperance, along with Faith, Hope, Charity, Prudence, Fortitude, and Justice, was depicted as an elegant, learned woman. Like most allegorical figures, she personified an abstract idea and possessed an identifying attribute. Temperance representing moderation, equilibrium, timing, and balance had as her symbolic, identifying device, a mechanical clock. Just as Justice was portrayed wielding her scales, Temperance was associated with the time-measuring technological marvel of gears and escapement mechanisms, which in turn exemplified perfect, active heavenly order. Giovanni da Dondi, a physician, astronomer, and clockmaker, created a magnificent clockwork in 1348 to measure hours, minutes, and planetary movements, representing the harmonies of the microcosm, the human body, with the macrocosm, the heavenly spheres in their orbits and rotations. Here Christine de Pizan teaches the power of temperance to four listening women. Her geared clock with an hour hand and a minute hand is surmounted by a bell for ringing the hours for prayer, for markets, and for life's ceremonial feasts.

Chivalry. Their quarrel concerning whose devotees ought to rule earthly affairs allows Christine to return as courier to her native France, below, for it to choose the wisest ruler.

Subtly insinuating local politics into moral discourse, Christine descends the ladder, ultimately landing in bed, awakened when her mother knocks on her bedroom door at morning. Christine's *Road of Long Studies* is such an allegory as she admired in the works of Deschamps, "subtle coverings, beautiful matter hidden under delectable fictions."

From Christine as early woman astronaut, let us go to Christine as city planner and master builder. Her *City of Ladies* is an awesome architectural, social, political, intellectual, and practical women's utopia. Women have power and control over all their actions in the City of Ladies, maintaining exact correspondences with social orders elsewhere dominated by men. Woman's power here is so free of masculine contribution or intrusion that the very buildings, from foundations dug by shovel and trowel to masonry walls aligned by rule and plumb line, all are built by

Christine herself accompanied by three supernatural collaborators, the three learned queens named Reason, Right Thinking, and Justice.

Probably the best-known of Christine's writings, the work is often misconstrued. It opens with a rash yearning: "Oh dear God I wish I had been born a man." This has been quoted as a medieval example of female self-hatred and penis-envy. In its context, however, the statement is a literary ploy not to state woman's gloom but to assert woman's glory. Reading antifeminist treatises in her office, Christine wonders whether God could have purposely made women evil. Otherwise bright-minded philosophers and poets seemed in those treatises to have achieved unanimity in condemning women. She cries, "Alas, good Lord, why have you not made me born into this world a man so that I should not have erred in anything and might be as greatly perfect as men say they are."

Reason, Right Thinking, and Justice arrive, and laughingly comfort her. They rescue her from this folly of thought. They help her build the

Opposite: *Women prophets called sibyls were known for predicting the future and writing books. One of the oldest and most popular in medieval art and literature was the Cumaean Sibyl, mentioned in Virgil's* Aeneid. *In negotiations with Tarquin, the Cumaean Sibyl insisted on selling her predictions for a high price. Tarquin refused, until systematically she burned her books one at a time until he relented, purchasing her final three books for the original asking price. Medieval Christian theologians admired a 15-book collection called the* Sibylline Oracles, *stunningly comprehensive world histories from the beginning of the world to the fall of Rome, apparently written by Jewish and Christian authors imitating pagan sibylline books. One book defends Jewish monotheism, another presents apocalyptic prophesies, another treats Jesus Christ's human and divine natures and his second birth. Monotheistic and messianic, the oracle collection was written in hexameters and used with enthusiasm by early church fathers. The books were retained at Rome for consultation during ecclesiastical emergencies. The Sibyls influenced the works of Clement of Alexandria, Theophilus of Antioch, Lactantius, and St. Augustine, who quoted the sibyls in his* City of God.

City of Ladies, the dwelling place for women of good repute. Their labors of architecture, design, masonry, stone-dressing, paving, vaulting, crenellation, and window-setting are relieved by numerous tales of women's excellences, and their achievements in warfare, government, education, and invention. Women are credited with inventing musical instruments, agricultural tools, armaments, the alphabet, and shorthand.

Why then do men vilify women? Christine de Pizan offers two answers. First is the heritage of Eve. In the Old Testament, Eve seduced men into sin, making all daughters share her guilt. Second, men hate women because of envy and jealousy: women are superior to men.

Among the tales the women city builders tell of miscellaneous heroines is that of the contemporary artist Anastasia. Christine knew her personally: she had hired her to illustrate her manuscripts. By a woman's fees so shall you know her achievements. Christine says that Anastasia is so skillful in painting manuscript marginalia and backgrounds of stories that though the most famous artists, the manuscript illuminators called the sovereign workmen of the world, live in Paris, she surpasses them all. She charges more for her labors than they charge for theirs. "I know by experience," says Christine, "for she has wrought for me many diverse things" for which Christine paid handsomely.

After the final tower of the City of Ladies is in place, who is to inhabit this site of woman's grace? Virtuous ladies are invited, heroines biblical, classical, and contemporary.

What about women not charter members who aspire to a place in the City of Ladies? For them Christine wrote another book, an instruction manual for right behavior for all classes of women from queens down to streetwalkers. Dedicated to Princess Margaret of Burgundy, the *Book of the Three Virtues or Mirror of Honor* is meant to inspire women and "to improve the welfare and honor of all women, be they great, middle class, or small." She offers advice to those living not in utopian female isolation, but in the world with men. She specifically addresses princesses who must rule their kingdoms with or without their husbands, and who must act as regents for their sons. She advises noble ladies who must rule their manors, caring for their large farms, castle households, and kitchens, account books, and security forces. She counsels townswomen, either independent craftswomen in the brewing, baking, and cloth trades, or responsible, rich wives of burgesses.

Christine instructs churchwomen to live active yet contemplative lives. She cautions widows to defend their financial rights and reaffirm personal independence. She counsels aging, wrinkling women not to condemn as immoral those pleasures of the young which they are now too old to indulge.

Christine addresses whores who suffer bad nights and blows from their clients. The *Book of Three Virtues* is a treasury of practical advice for the thinking, active, practical woman of daily affairs who must exercise responsibility justly for the greatest good of her nation, her town, her family, and herself.

Christine de Pizan celebrated women, challenged, inspired, praised, and chastised them. Her well-tempered feminism does not deny the possibilities for happiness with *man*kind. She had lived happily with a man. But, she suggests, neither loving a man nor being loved by a man requires one to stop loving oneself, honoring one's own talents, or working according to one's own highest standards.

Christine de Pizan was a forceful, gracious feminist. She was perfectly tuned to the emotional pitches of both men and women. Popular among male patrons who paid her generously for excellent work, she also pleased female patrons. Christine balanced righteous anger against men's misogyny with humane understanding and compassion. She articulately refuted woman-haters, and she precisely devastated the arguments of those men who exploit widows, or wives, or any talented woman.

Christine de Pizan also was thoroughly good-natured. She instructed, encouraged, and ultimately aggrandized women. As a professional woman she transformed personal adversity into opportunity, sharpening her expertise on the stone of necessity. Fair to other women and fair to men, she argued against detractors convincingly and cogently. Yet she maintained equilibrium between learned excellence and popular appeal. She used the literary conventions her audience loved. She produced for her market. It willingly paid her. People admiringly complained that she was one of the most expensive writers in France. She achieved literary fortune and fame while maintaining an affable vigor, a compassionate strength, a gentle formidability.

MARGUERITE DE NAVARRE

Last of the four formidable female writers is Marguerite de Navarre, noblewoman, friend, and colleague of both Montaigne and Rabelais.

Playwright, poet, and moralist, Marguerite is best known for her *Heptameron*. Modeled in part upon Boccaccio's *Decameron,* it is a group of 72 tales told by a diverse, delightful gathering of 10 men and women probably modeled upon her own family and friends. Marguerite de Navarre herself takes the part of Parlemente, one of the storytelling *devisants* occupying themselves while forced to take sanctuary in a monastery.

The stories are brilliant. The 10 characters' comments after the tales provide analytical jewels of philosophy and historical realism. A modern reader may have some trouble with her prose style: it is prolix. She wrote some of the longest run-on sentences in the 16th century, possibly because she dictated to a scribe while traveling. Nevertheless Marguerite de Navarre's stories inexorably lead along a brambly path to the later European novel.

The Rabelaisian erotic humor of Marguerite de Navarre's tales depends upon wit and pun. Double and triple meanings to seemingly innocent words bring a blush to even the most experienced readers of medieval and Renaissance smut. Here is one brief example, which plays with exuberant vulgarity on the 16th-century phrase in France for winnowing basket, the agricultural implement which separates seed from chaff. The phrase, *van à vanner,* could also mean the human anatomical vessel through which seed penetrates, the vagina.

A rich old farmer married a beautiful young woman with whom he had no children. She made up for his lack by having many good friends. When she wore out the gentlemen and people of quality, she turned to her last resort, the church, taking as companion in sin one who could absolve her for it, her priest. A potent shepherd, he often came to play with his lamb. They acted their mystery play secretly.

When the husband one day came home from work unexpectedly early, the priest had no chance to escape. So he climbed into the attic above, covering the hole with a winnowing basket. After the doddering old husband had eaten and drunk heavily and had fallen asleep in his chair by the fire, the priest looked out from the hole above, stretching his neck as far as he could. He thrust so hard on the winnowing basket, that winnowing basket and man came tumbling down in front of the sleeping husband.

Scrambling to his feet, the priest said, "Here, good neighbor, is your winnowing basket. Many thanks." The wife said to her old husband, "The priest borrowed your winnowing basket and has come to return it."

The old farmer grumbled, "That's a rude way to return a winnowing basket."

Exemplary women writers, Countess de Dia, Marie de France, Christine de Pizan, and Marguerite de Navarre were among the fine professional women of the medieval and Renaissance world who lived not by their work alone, but by their work, mostly.

MEDICAL WOMEN: PHYSICIANS, SURGEONS, AND PHARMACISTS

The magnificent heritage of the medical women of the Middle Ages is hidden. Medical treatises, laws, court documents, depictions of women practitioners in literature and art, commendations and criticisms by their medieval contemporaries are unequivocal, unassailable data. Yet before we can celebrate medieval medical women we must first break through a pervasive modern assumption that they never existed.

Otherwise dependable medical and legal historians are willing to acknowledge their existence, but only as charlatans, quacks, superstitious "old wives" and midwives, not as respected, licensed physicians and surgeons. At a recent bar association meeting on medical malpractice litigation, a medieval medical malpractice case was introduced as the historic predecessor to a current case in California. A prominent lawyer in the audience sententiously said, "Medieval medical women's practices *were* malpractices. Women never were granted licenses to practice." He quoted, correctly, a law from the archives of London, dated 1390. "No unlicensed woman shall be allowed to practice surgery within the boundaries

Opposite: Women physicians and women nurses treated patients at home as well as in clinics and hospitals. Bearing pain patiently, with the stoic acceptance of the biblical Job, was earthly proof of a person's ability to accept God's divine will. Illness and injury were thought to have triple uses beyond mere accident: to punish the sinning, to purge sinners of their sins, and to prove the virtue of the saintly. Popular philosophical and medical texts as well as learned theological treatises counseled patience in pain and physical adversity. Illness exemplified the paired opposites of acting and waiting, doing and suffering, agere et pati *(Latin, "to do and to suffer"), two opposites of the human condition. Experiences either were initiated and acted or received and endured. People either were actors or patients. This patient, provoked by a winged, mocking devil hiding beneath his bed, kicks over his medicine table, and with his skinny left leg kicks out a cowl-hooded physician. Despite the patient's wrath, the medical women patiently persist, one serving him medicinal foods, in the foreground, while the other, gesticulating in the background, counsels reason and patience. Dying well was hard work. Instruction books titled* Ars Moriendi *(Art of dying) taught how to exit from the world beautifully.*

of the City of London. Unlicensed practitioners are a danger to their patients, to the reputation of the profession, and to the citizenry."

The law states that. But that law also prevents unlicensed *men* from practicing within the bounds of the city. It insists, as do numerous earlier and later laws and regulations, that master surgeons examine both the skills and credentials of all potential practitioners, native or foreign, male or female, before a license is granted. Furthermore, the law requires each practitioner treating a patient in danger of serious injury or death to obtain a consultation from a master specialist.

Fourteenth-century London's civil authority, in conjunction with the medical and surgical guilds, examined its medical practitioners for skill and education, licensed them, required expert consultation and peer review in cases of morbid or mortal danger, disciplined malefactors, and required physicians and surgeons to provide financial sureties in a prototype of medical malpractice insurance. Medieval medical legislation and the litigation demonstrate responsible control over medical practice, with definitive rights and responsibilities ascribed to the patients, the men and women physicians and surgeons, the guilds, the government, and the citizenry.

The reasons why licensed women physicians and surgeons are thought not to have existed in the Middle Ages are complicated. Simone de Beauvoir recognized that the history of women has been written by men, but this does not fully explain the disappearance of medieval medical women. Estimable women scholars, as well as men, examining straightforward, valid historical documents, condemn the achievements of medical women to legend, so powerful is the influence of their prejudices and expectations. Modern inheritors of the Victorian ethos smother medieval medical women's achievements under the clutter of 19th-century sexual proprieties.

An illustrated medieval treatise on warfare, for example, depicts battlefield surgeons treating the wounded at the front lines. Three practitioners stand on the battlements of a besieged castle, performing surgery while the fight rages. One doctor removes an arrow from a nobleman's face wound. Of the three medical figures, one is male, and two definitively are female.

Modern captions to this illustration insist that a surgeon (male) is operating and two nurses (female) assist. But the medieval manuscript describes three doctors. Such surgical teams were common on medieval battlefields. Skilled itinerant women surgeons traveled from battle to battle healing the wounded. A typical document dated 1394 in the German archives of Frankfurt records fees to Dr. Barbara, a Jewish woman physician, for attending the battle-injured at Wissenkirchen.

Examining medical malfeasance is one of the best ways to understand historical medical excellence. Medical malpractice documents provide especially intriguing evidence of the state of medieval medical women's art. In law courts patients sued physicians and surgeons for excessive fees, ineffective cures, or new complications based on medical interventions, the *iatrogenic sequelae*. Sometimes physicians brought civil actions against other physicians. Malpractice testimonies are more comprehensive and dependable than theoretical disquisitions. Malpractice data allow modern perception not only of what might have been, but a four-part perception of what actually was: what the patient expected, what the practitioner promised, what the court resolved after peer review by the medical and surgical guilds, and what the city or national government required under its laws.

To set the medieval medical context for women practitioners, here is a brief composite portrait derived from documents from the 11th through 15th centuries depicting women in medical practice, and their expertise in the equivalents of such modern specialties as surgery, obstetrics, gynecology, medical pharmacology, ophthalmology, battlefield trauma surgery, chronic disease care, and treatment of contagious diseases. Women also worked as medical anatomists and pathologists, writers of medical textbooks, and medical school professors. Eleventh-century Dr. Trotula of Salerno and 12th-century Dr. Hildegard of Bingen, who is better known today as a composer and poet, and venerated as if a saint, were notable medical theorists and practitioners whose writings repay scrupulous study.

Medical women ministered to men and women patients at all junctures between birth and death. Attending the needs of pregnant women of all social classes, medieval women obstetricians were constantly in demand and often highly paid. The physician Marjorie Cobb received a handsome annuity for attending Queen Elizabeth, the wife of King Edward IV, in 1470.

OBSTETRICS AND GYNECOLOGY

An obstetric and gynecological text written by the 11th-century woman physician and medical school professor Dr. Trotula of Salerno was titled *De passionibus mulieres, On Women's Diseases.* It reviews normal and complicated births.

After prenatal preparations by diet therapy and exercise, the medical women direct the patient in labor to a practical, functional position, seated on a birth stool. While forces of gravity and natural contraction aid the babe's passage through the birth canal, the woman squats as comfortably as could be reasonably expected on the chair. Obstetricians and midwives kneel or hunker down in front of the patient. Physicians encourage the woman's participation visually and tactually in the birth of her child.

The newly born medieval babe, before being given to the mother to hold, is carefully washed and anointed with medicated ointments and salves, while being checked for healthy eyes, and, as Trotula instructs, a tongue tie (which the doctor would cut), straight limbs, and firm joints.

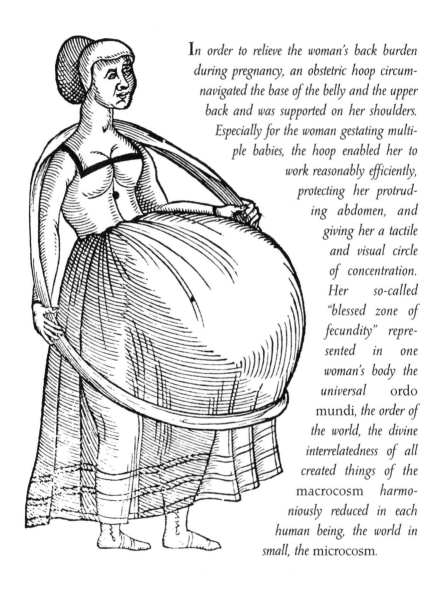

In order to relieve the woman's back burden during pregnancy, an obstetric hoop circumnavigated the base of the belly and the upper back and was supported on her shoulders. Especially for the woman gestating multiple babies, the hoop enabled her to work reasonably efficiently, protecting her protruding abdomen, and giving her a tactile and visual circle of concentration. Her so-called "blessed zone of fecundity" represented in one woman's body the universal ordo mundi, the order of the world, the divine interrelatedness of all created things of the macrocosm harmoniously reduced in each human being, the world in small, the microcosm.

To maintain the baby's posture as well as its warmth and comfort, the obstetrician wraps the child in swaddling bands or blankets. To prevent accidental suffocation, infants are not to sleep in bed with their mothers, but in a cradle nearby.

Medieval obstetricians and midwives suggest ingenious practical methods for difficult and complicated deliveries. Cesarean section is indicated for the woman with a narrow, injured, or deformed pelvis. After surgical incision in the side wall of the abdomen, the baby is removed head first.

The physician and women attendants note the exact moment of delivery. Paintings of birth scenes often depict a round object above the mother's head and pillow: a convex mirror registering the view through a window of the position of the stars and moon in the night sky. Proper plotting of constellations will indicate the zodiacal sign of the infant, and genethlialogy, the art of birth forecasting, predicts its probable physique, temperament, personality, and future profession.

An individual fetus in a dangerous birth position and multiple babes present particular obstetric hazards. Following the earlier Greek obstetrician Soranus's recommendations, Dr. Trotula describes how babies may be turned in the uterus, how safely to induce labor, how to handle breach and hazardous delivery positions, and how to protect mother and child postpartum.

Intriguing obstetric medicinal and mechanical devices used by medieval medical women were derived from Greek, Latin, and Arabic sources, often mediated to western Europe by Jewish translators. To stimulate faster contractions during protracted labor, a preparation of coriander seed was inserted at the vagina. To hasten delivery in long labor, medical midwives adapted the Roman technique of bouncing the patient on a jogging table. Surgical procedures women obstetricians performed included episiotomy, replacement of a prolapsed uterus, and, as Dr. Trotula of Salerno's treatise on surgery of the perineum recommends, specific surgical sewings plus medicated tampons, herbal compresses, and hygienic douches. An admirer of Trotula, the physician Constantine the African, reports her handling a dramatic case of vulval abscess which all other physicians misdiagnosed and mistreated until Trotula, *magistra operis,* master surgeon, operated successfully.

Medieval medical women treated difficulties of dysmenorrhea and menopause with hot water bottles, baths, gymnastics, medicinal herbs and spices in pills, foods, and drinks, steaming the vulva, and intravaginal fumigations. For pain from intestinal or genital cancer, women practitioners gave analgesics, soporifics, and anesthetics, taken most often by inhaling vapors from heated opium, hyoscyamus, hemlock, or mandrake. Breast abscesses and cancers were treated by medicine, herbal compress, or mastectomy. In theory and practice, many medieval women practitioners seem to have shared Dr. Trotula of Salerno's compassionate expertise: "I, Trotula, pitying the calamities of women, and at the urgent request of certain ones, write this book on the diseases which affect the female sex."

MEN AND WOMEN PATIENTS

Women physicians, however, did not treat only women patients. A 13th-century English physician named Agnes, the Medica, received a valuable grant of land and income from the Abbot of Thorney. This English female practitioner who received payment from a monastery was apparently one of its attending physicians. Medical women frequently treated monks. A physician named Johannah, for example, in 1408 made numerous visits to heal two monks in Westminster Abbey. The Infirmarer's Rolls record payments to Dr. Johannah over a period of two years for medications for Brother William Ashwell and Brother Richard Merlaw. Lest anyone believe that this name Johannah is a scribal error for a male doctor named John, one entry lists the fee of 3 shillings, 6 pence for medication paid to Johannah, physician, mulieri, the lady doctor.

Surprising numbers of medieval medical women practiced eye surgery. Of these, many were Jewish. Rabbi Judah Ben Asher, dying in Toledo, Spain, in 1349, recounted his experience with two Jewish ophthalmologists who treated his near blindness. The first who tried to cure him failed. The second doctor treated him for two months before she herself died. "Had she lived," said the Rabbi, "I would have regained my eyesight fully. If she had not treated me, I would never have seen again. Blest be God for her. She showed me His wonders and opened my eyes to see the works of His hands."

Numerous female eye doctors appear among the lists of *Juden-Ercztin,* Jewish physicians, in the archives of Frankfurt-on-Main. So skillful were these female occultist-surgeons that they were said to operate more

Three workers in a distillery prepare medications and culinary additives from grains and vegetables stacked on the shelves behind the woman, at left, who sorts kernels from chaff. The woman, at right, pours a liquid from one thin-mouthed flask into a Florence flask through a funnel or strainer. The man tends the furnaces, heating substances in distilling devices called cucurbits, *alembics, and* pelicans. *Heat is generated in two ways, via an open fire in a large open hearth, at left, and in an enclosed furnace resembling an* athenor, *the furnaces used by alchemists and metallurgists to maintain a high, constant heat.*

quickly than one can describe the operations. Speed was a blessing during surgery without general anesthesia.

Women physicians and practitioners of medical pharmacology compounded medicines and salves in their offices or worked professionally in laboratories surrounded by distillation chambers, retorts, flasks, and separating chambers. Such a noble woman physician as Dorothea was lauded by her patients for successful cures with medications she compounded herself.

Women physicians recommended herbal and mineral medications for problems of sexuality—too much of it, or not enough. Certain animals and fish were thought to be sexual stimulants. To prevent menstruation and conception, women drank decoctions of fennel or acorn steeped in wine. Men, to increase sperm production, potency, and fertility, drank aphrodisiac wines fermented from turnips, artichokes, or leeks.

Women pharmacologists recommended oil of bitter almonds mixed with butter rubbed into the skin as a soothing cleansing ointment. For

Opposite: Four women bathe a knight outdoors in a warm bath. A long-haired woman presents the naked man a footed chalice of wine while a hooded woman servitor squats down before the fire to stimulate it with bellows, heating a cauldron for the portable wooden tub's hot water strewn with fragrant flowers, medicinal herbs, and leaves. On her knees in front of the tub, another woman, wearing a reticula (a bejeweled hairnet covering her hair), massages the man's right arm above and below his elbow. Balding in front with hair curling at his neck behind, he is ready to be crowned with a chaplet, a garland of flowers. Therapeutic baths in homes, cottages, and castles were augmented by popular public baths and health spas throughout Europe in the 13th through 15th centuries. People traveled from afar to health spas. Local entrepreneurs and physicians profited from natural hot springs, from artificially heated pools and baths, from mineral-laden natural springs, and from indoor and outdoor pools to which minerals, spices, and fragrant herbs, thought to have specific medicinal effect, were added. Their commercial success remains today in names of the towns in which they thrived, such as Bath in England, Baden-Baden in Germany, and Spa, near Liège, in Belgium.

superfluous facial hair or pimples Dr. Trotula of Salerno suggested aloes boiled in rosewater. She also had splendid recipes for sunburn cream, scalp oil, hair dyes, lipstick, rouge, gargles, deodorizing mouthwashes (one pleasant to taste is made from honey, cucumbers, and water), hand softeners (asphodel mixed with egg white), hair perfume ("all noble Salernitan men and women delight in fragrance of musk in the hair"), and a strawberry and herb deodorant for hirsismus or stinking armpits.

Yet other medieval medical women treated chronic diseases. Some worked in leprosy isolation hospitals, the leprosaria. Women practitioners also were hired by town health authorities as searchers in times of plague. These women dared the danger of infection by examining patients suspected of having bubonic or pneumonic plague, also risking revilement and physical attack: positive diagnosis of plague meant the patients' quarantine. Since the entire household was quarantined, economic ruin for the family generally followed the searchers posting the

sign of pestilence on the door, and the searchers could become the focus of the family's distress.

Medical women also practiced in health spas. Popular medical manuals such as the *Tacuinum Sanitatis* recommend the healing powers of water for soaking wounds and stimulating painful stiff joints. Phlebotomy or bloodletting was one of the services offered at spas. It was practiced by fleaming (lancing a vein with a scalpel), cupping (placing vacuum cups upon skin incisions to draw blood), or leeching (applying live blood suckers). Other medieval bath practitioners helped in erotic water therapies. Hydrotherapy treatises maintained that thwarted sexuality was bad for mental health. So spas often provided the aphrodisiac drinks and sensual waters to lubricate the voluptuaries' passage from bath to bed.

Women searchers and physicians also were hired to ferret out causes of death. Working with municipal coroners' offices (which existed in London in the 12th century), with sheriffs, town mayors, or criminal courts, women investigated suspicious deaths, checking corpses for signs of criminal negligence, poison, or murder.

Medical women performed autopsies. Although we tend to think otherwise, human dissections certainly were performed in the Middle Ages for forensic purposes and for anatomical studies. Laws prohibiting dissections were created because dissections were common. Medieval legal prohibitions of autopsy probably prevented it just as well as prohibition of adultery guaranteed that no man or woman had sex outside marriage. Likewise, the sacred commandment "do not kill" did not keep nations free of violence, murder, or war. Women anatomists worked with the famous Mondino de Luzzi in the 1490s, examining organs, bones, and blood vessels of cadavers.

MEDICAL LICENSES

Among these varied medical women's practices, many women were validly licensed practitioners. Many were not. Medical licensure is a tricky subject. Depending upon the century and the city, medical and surgical licenses were granted to men and women by town authorities, by medical guilds, by university faculties, by the country's king, or by a powerful churchman such as a bishop. Just as American medical practitioners must obtain specific state licenses, so medieval local areas granted or refused medical privileges for practice after testing candidates.

Medical licensing, medieval and modern, regulates numbers of practitioners, controls competition among them, and, theoretically, governs the quality of health care by requiring minimum standards of education and practical experience, by promulgating medical standards, by requiring adherence to them, by preventing violations, and by punishing medical malpractice.

Women physicians and surgeons were licensed throughout medieval Europe. Some licenses were granted by the usual city or state authorities. Some women physicians sought licenses from unexpected sources: a Jew from an archbishop, and an English widow from the King himself.

The British Public Record Office, for example, preserves a petition from the early 1400s by the woman physician Joan, widow of William du Lee, to King Henry IV for "License to practice medicine [*physic*] about the country without hindrance by all folk who despise her by reason of her said art."

In Sicily the Jewish woman physician Virdimura was examined by royal court physicians in 1376 and granted permission to practice medicine throughout the kingdom because "of the praise universally bestowed upon her."

Dr. Sarah of Wurzburg, a Jew, petitioned Archbishop John II to grant her a license to practice medicine throughout his German bishopric. So granted, the document dated 1419 reads: "Concerning Sarah, the Jewish doctor franchised for the past three years, we agree she is to pay annual taxes and for the next three full years to practice her profession without interference, unconditionally; should anyone prosecute her, we will take action against such one, unconditionally." Sarah must have had a lucrative practice. A court document signed by the entire Franconian nobility grants her the vast lands, properties, and the whole estate of one Friedrich von Riedern of the bishopric of Franconia.

Licensing physicians and surgeons in order to avoid malpractice goes back at least to the 12th century. In 1190 King Roger insisted that to maintain the excellence of the medical craft in Salerno, Italy, all practitioners must be examined before being licensed. Holy Roman Emperor Frederick II, king of Sicily, in 1240 reaffirmed such licensing strictures. Since so many medical practitioners of Salerno were women, doubtlessly they were licensed, or not, just as male practitioners were. However only legislation exists, and there are no known law court cases describing medical women's licensed or unlicensed activities in Salerno.

Medical women in France and England certainly were expected to obtain medical licenses. When they did not, no matter how excellent or deficient their craft, they were accused of malpractice. Blurring distinctions between intentional medical negligence and charlatanism on the one hand, and simple practice without license on the other, the University of Paris medical faculty was particularly vigorous in prosecuting in the courts both women and men. Female practitioners are accused of malpractice just as men are; their professional actions equally examined by university interrogators after testimony of expert witnesses; their alleged malfeasances are judged identically; if guilty, their punishments are equivalent.

To control health care quality, that University of Paris medical faculty entered an ingenious coalition with city and church authorities. Anyone convicted of medical malpractice in 13th-century France risked not only such civil punishments as fines or jail or banning from practice, but also excommunication from the church and public denunciation by priests from their pulpits in Paris.

Stringent regulations established in 1271 were supported by the bishop of Paris, by royal authority, and by the University of Paris faculty of medicine. These rules limit types of surgery, medical ministrations, and pharmaceutical responsibilities considered legal for both male and female practitioners. Later, however, popes, professors, and kings complain in monotonous litany about substandard and illegal medical practices, many of which include allegations against women practitioners. In 1325 the pope rails against people ignorant of the medical art, particularly certain "old women." Five years later, in 1330, he still writes agitated letters to the bishop of Paris and the University against medical malpractitioners.

Reversing the compliment, the dean and faculty of the University of Paris medical division in 1347 petition the pope against "men and women audaciously usurping the office of physician, engaging in medical practice about which they know little or nothing." King John of France laments in a royal edict of 1352 that unauthorized persons of both sexes are dispensing drugs and medicines freely in Paris, particularly certain women, as well as monks. Thus for the welfare of his subjects, he forbids anyone of either sex "to administer any medicine, alterative, electuary, laxative pills or clysters of any sort" for symptoms that he or she does not understand. Nor may any man or woman administer opiates or give medical advice unless already a University master or licentiate in medicine or otherwise approved as qualified to practice. Neither king nor pope, neither bishop nor university alone could reform medical practice in Paris. Practitioners of both sexes could be licensed and were.

Law in medieval Paris also regulated women pharmacists. A statute of 1322 required men and women apothecaries to administer medication under the jurisdiction of master physicians; to swear to follow a corrected copy of the poison antidote text, the *Antidotarium* of Nicholas of Salerno; to measure their medications by accurate weight; to use only pure medications in their prescriptions; and to substitute no medications for those prescribed other than those listed in the *quid pro quo,* the alphabetical table of drugs and their substitutes.

MEDICAL MALPRACTICE CASES

Medical women were sometimes brought to court for violating medical licensing strictures and for actual malpractice. Clarice de Rothomago's case exemplifies the ineffectiveness of these rules against successful though unlicensed practitioners. Along with her physician husband, Peter Faverel, Clarice de Rothomago was accused of illegally practicing in Paris. She was arrested, tried, and excommunicated by the Bishop's Court as well as denounced in the churches of Paris.

She appealed her case, bringing to court a long stream of witnesses attesting to her successful cures. Though again condemned, she continued practicing. Her patients apparently preferred the woman physician who cured their ailments to the rules of university and church.

In another woman physician's medical malpractice case, Dr. Jacqueline Felicia de Almenia was brought to court in 1322, and not for the first time, for practicing medicine in Paris without a medical license. This remarkable doctor, said to be of noble birth, probably German, and 30 years old in the year 1322, defended herself eloquently and elegantly. Witnesses testified to her remarkable skill as both diagnostician and practitioner.

Dr. Jacqueline Felicia cured where licensed practitioners failed. Naming the unsuccessful doctors, both men and women patients insisted that master physicians such as Gilbert, Herman, Manfred, and Thomas could do nothing. But once the good woman doctor had palpated pulse, testing its music, and examined urine, she prescribed a potion, an *aquam clarissimam,* whose effectiveness proved remarkable. Patient after patient referred to this "clearest water" cure.

Dr. Jacqueline Felicia testified brilliantly, reminding the court that the law was established to eliminate foolish, fatuous, ignorant practitioners rather than excellent physicians such as herself, who were well educated, experienced, and expert in practice. She concluded with a stirring call for more sagacious, expert women to treat female patients, arguing that women practitioners see and treat certain diseases which women patients will not permit men physicians to examine. Many women prefer to die rather than reveal their secret illnesses; but were it possible to be examined by one of their own sex they would be cured. *Mulier sapienta, discreta, et experta*—a wise, discreet, and expert woman practitioner—could restore harmony between human and heavenly bodies, thus preventing unnecessary deaths. Jacqueline Felicia presented herself as just such a woman medical practitioner.

A particularly horrific malpractice accusation against a woman demonstrates how common women medical practitioners were. In 15th-century Italy there practiced a remarkable Jewish woman physician

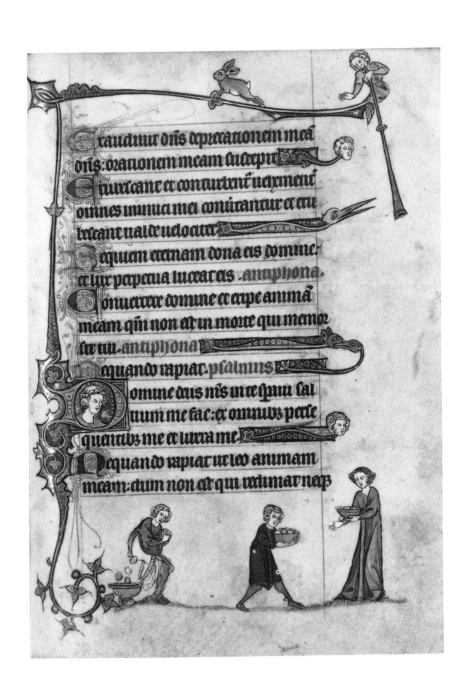

Opposite: Urinanalysis and feces analysis were diagnostic tools for determining disease or injury before treatment and before prognosis. With his pants down, exposing his bare behind, a man defecates light green eggs into a gold toilet bowl. An attendant gathers the feces and conveys a bowlful to the woman for study. She probably is a physician, wearing a typical 14th-century medical robe. Her hair is covered with a reticulated headdress. Both urine and feces were examined for color, odor, sedimentation, presence or absence of occult blood, and undigested items and chemicals. The attributes of Saints Cosmos and Damian, the patron saints of medicine and surgery, are a urine flask for uroscopy and a feces box for feces analysis. To modern eyes a bizarre decoration in a private prayer book, such juxtapositions of the sacred and the profane were commonplaces of medieval life and art. Scatological images in the margins of Gothic manuscripts had the effect of humor but also demonstrated the fundamental variety and bountiful plenty of the created universe. Everything human, including eating, urination, defecation, and coitus, was occasion for observation, analysis, and art, and for praising the Maker who created them.

named Brunetta. In a virulently anti-Semitic denunciation of Dr. Brunetta, the powerful Bernadius of Siena complained that as a physician she gained dangerous access into Christian homes and even intruded upon Christian councils.

Dr. Brunetta, along with fellow Jews, was the accused in a court trial which resulted in the condemnation of the Jewish community of Trent and its complete annihilation. They were accused and convicted of ritual blood guilt. The court made the horrible accusation that Jews use a Christian child's life blood at the spring holiday of Passover to bake matzos.

The Jews of Trent were found guilty of killing young Simon of Trent. Brunetta was specifically charged with furnishing the needles to draw out the boy's blood. The fact that she was singled out for this hateful charge is powerful indirect evidence that she was an important and trusted physician in Trent.

LITERARY LADY DOCTORS

Literature provides as intriguing evidence for medical women as does law. The 12th-century tale by Marie de France called the *Lai of the Two Lovers* presents a king so possessive of his beautiful daughter that he imposed an impossible task on all her suitors desiring marriage. A woman physician plays a vital part in their tragic story.

As test of strength and proof of devotion, the king required each prince desiring the princess to carry her up a steep mountain in his arms. None having the requisite stamina, countless disappointed lovers rolled down the hill in defeat. However, the young princess herself planned a clever stratagem to help her true beloved win her according to her father's outrageous demands.

In addition to starving herself to make his burden lighter, she suggested that her lover go to her aunt in Salerno, a physician who practiced medicine and knew the secret gifts of every root and herb. From her he obtained not only counsel but cure: a "cunning" herb that would strengthen his body and comfort his heart. With such a potion strengthening limbs and resolve, he would easily carry her up the perilous mountain without rest.

Traveling to Italy, the lover brought back that magic medicine, and he carried it with him and his lady up the mountain. But because of his courage and youthful impetuousness, he refused the benevolent drink. Staggering with his beloved to the summit, his heart could not stand the exertion. He sprawled dead.

The princess in sorrow and doleful passion flung her body on his and died of grief. The stimulating potion from the woman physician of Salerno now being strewn upon the ground, a fine garden of medicinal herbs has grown there since that day.

A literary lady doctor of another sort appears in the racy 13th-century fabliau called "The Lady Doctor," "*La Saineresse.*" A superb tale with double meanings in every line, it epitomizes the way in which a wily wife will deceive her husband in order to indulge her sexual exuberance.

A rich old man foolishly boasted that a woman could never deceive him. His wife, swearing to make a liar of him without his knowing it, arranged for her handsome noble lover to come to her home while her husband and she were there together. Dressing himself as a woman physician in a loose robe and a fine saffron yellow wimple, the lover brought bleeding cups for medicinal phlebotomy. He greeted the rich old man enthusiastically and the beautiful young wife. Summoning her disguised lover upstairs to the bedroom, she said to her husband, "I have need of this physician's craft for I have a most wondrous pain in my thighs. Because of that I must be bled a bit."

Up she went, closed the door, and she and her lover immediately seized one another. They stretched on the bed and they coupled three times. Thus they played, coupled, kissed, and hugged, and then came downstairs *en fin,* at last.

The husband said to his wife, "Pay this lady doctor well for her services." The wife suggested she has already cared for that business, yet brought a purse to a lady doctor.

To his wife who was still quite out of breath, the husband said, "Lady, you are all flushed. You stayed up there too long."

"Yes, by God, I have been overworked. I could not be bled. No matter how many times she would strike there, not a drop of blood came forth. Three times in succession that one took me. Each time she placed upon my thighs two of her tools and so struck me that I was completely martyred. Those heavy repeated strokes might have killed me if it had not been for a good ointment. She who has this ointment is not tormented with pain. She anointed my wounds, which were large and wide, so well that I am completely cured. That ointment issues forth from a pipe, descends into an opening with a very black and hairy covering, which is *savoreuse,* savory sweet indeed."

Extravagantly, joyously vulgar, this cuckolding could not be so crude were it not for the prevalence in town and country of the lady doctor making house calls.

MYSTERIOUS VANISHINGS OF MEDICAL WOMEN

Many scholars consider the medieval woman physician Trotula of Salerno a legendary figure. If she existed at all, she is thought to be a superstitious "old wife" who peddled herbs and remedies to country believers. A charlatan and an unlearned empiric, silly old Dame Trot was a midwife and a fool. Books attributed to Trot, *Trotula major* and *Trotula minor,* were written by a man. Women physicians such as Trotula did not exist. Trotula was a man.

Remarkably, Bernard of Provins, professor at Salerno around 1150, incorporated huge sections of Trotula's works into his medical treatise and praised her as a woman physician. Peter of Spain, who became Pope John XXI in 1276, was so excited about Trotula's work that for his *Thesaurus Pauperum* he borrowed voluminously, enthusiastically quoting her remedies with his own notation: *Hoc ego,* I agree.

From her own days in the 11th century through the 16th, there was no question whether she existed, whether she was a woman, or whether she wrote the books attributed to her. As late as 1544, John Scottus, who printed her *Gynecology* in Strassburg, introduced her as a great and learned woman, a nigh universal opinion for half a millennium. For five hundred years Trotula unquestionably *was.*

But something happened on her way to today. No mere legendary reputation, Trotula herself became a legend. In the early modern period, critics wrote: "Trotula is no longer believed to be a woman and we have to judge the women of Salerno mainly by what others say of them." So says Thorndike. "Trotula and the women doctors of the University of Salerno in the eleventh and twelfth centuries are mythical figures, rapidly melting away under the cruel searchlight of modern research." So says Eileen Power. Trotula herself is now not considered to be a real person. "The name came to be attached to a compilation by one Trotus of Salerno, a male." So says M. M. Postam. The women doctors of Salerno must be condemned as "mythical," so say the editors of Hastings Rashdall.

A 12th-century churchman Orderic Vitalis praised a man as "so skilled in medicine that in Salerno, the ancient seat of the best medical schools, no one could equal him except one very learned woman." His 20th-century editor writes "This lady may have been legendary." What made Trotula disappear under the cruel white light of early modern research? Who was shining that searchlight?

A careless scribe in one manuscript wrote the masculine name Trottus instead of Trotula, thereby depriving the good medical professor not only of her chair but her identity. But the scribe's slip was only a beginning. Early this century, the attack on Trotula was formidable, one scholar particularly directing his scornful Victorian vision against her works. Professor Charles Singer emphasized two points: First, not only is there no autograph manuscript written by the author, but in the earliest manuscripts there are numerous versions of the author's name: Trotula, Trotta, Trocta, and in that one 11th-century manuscript, the masculine form of the name, Trottus. Second, there is no extant "original" Trotula work, for each version has some additions and accretions making it difficult to know exactly what was the archetype.

Surely it is not surprising that a popular Latin work translated to vernacular languages has name changes. A work by Johanus would belong to John in England, Jean in France, Juan in Spain, and in Italy, Giovanni. Furthermore, even excellent scribes occasionally nodded at their parchments, carelessly adding or omitting a quill stroke, making the difference between a masculine or feminine ending of a word.

Second, popular medieval works on so critical a subject as health usually have additions or deletions, and even contradictions. Each redactor or each physician might add an element which might offer the reader an extension of life against death's imperatives.

Clues to why Trotula incurred the ire of late Victorian critics are found in two comments by men who recognized she was a woman but expected her to possess a Victorian woman's modesty and sensibility. A Latin notation in an elaborate 18th-century hand, in the margin of an early printed edition which I studied in the British Museum, reads: "The woman author of this book I praise as a woman. Many things here recorded demonstrate the attempt of a woman to help her sex, which must have been foreign to her natural modesty to write, but which are honest business of a refined and gentle medical woman for the good of her sex."

And in an 1891 *History of Medical Education*, Puschmann reminds us that Trotula discusses all branches of pathology, even the diseases of the male sexual organs—a truly painful subject for female sensibility. (Doubtlessly the subject was somewhat more painful to her male patients.)

Perhaps if Trotula had not written so definitively on the diseases of the genitalia; if she had not written so reasonably and brilliantly on the female's perineum; and if she had not written so learnedly and practically on male sterility and painful penis dyscrasias, then she still might be thought to exist. For she would not be violating early modern expectations of woman's work.

Dr. Trotula of Salerno deserves the same courtesy we extend to medieval males: to appreciate the person or the art in medieval context. Let Dr. Trotula of Salerno be seen in the context of other medieval women healers. We may thus restore to her that appreciative wonderment which was her medieval and Renaissance legacy.

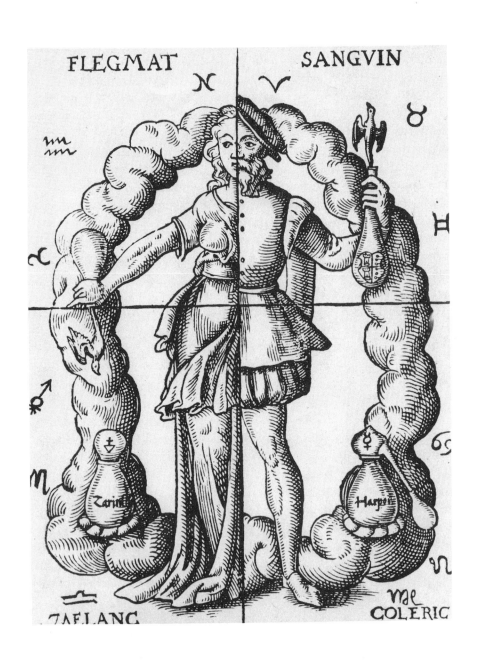

FLEGMAT   SANGVIN

ZAELANC   COLERIC

HILDEGARD OF BINGEN

Our last woman physician was so successful in her cures that people thought her achievements miracles and they judged her a saint. Hildegard of Bingen was a 12th-century churchwoman, abbess, poet, composer, writer of remarkable medical and natural historical texts, and leader of a large German nunnery. A visionary and mystic, Dr. Hildegard of Bingen was appreciated by St. Thomas à Becket as well as by her contemporary St. Bernard of Clairvaux. So popular was Hildegard for her cures as well as her visions that she was called the Christian Sibyl of the Rhine.

Her scientific and medical treatises are at once typical of 12th-century thought and startlingly original in practical detail.

Though her own contemporaries cheered her practical medical successes and clamored for her writings; though a 12th-century biography

Opposite: A hermaphrodite with gown-covered breast and hairless face, on the left, and tunic-clad body with bearded face, on the right, carries alchemical symbols and is surrounded by a continuous chemical plume from retorts, flasks, cucurbits *and* alembics *cooking medicines, chemicals, and metallurgical substances. The four* Temperaments, *phlegmatic, sanguine, choleric, and melancholic, were thought to be caused by an astrologically determined balance among the four bodily fluids, the* Humors, *and a preponderance, respectively, of phlegm, blood, yellow bile, and black bile. Related are the four essential qualities of physical matter, namely, hot, cold, moist, and dry, which characterize also the four elements out of which the universe is crafted: earth, air, fire, and water. Everything relates to everything and to everyone; each element in the great created order, the* ordo mundi, *shares qualities, purposes, and effects. Perturbations in the heavens cause bodily fevers and infirmities. Foods and drinks possessing inherent heat and moisture balance or counteract coldness and dryness in people's physical constitutions. Rational science developed from alchemy's attempts to understand natural order and natural law in the observed, intelligently contemplated world.*

specifically states that she wrote the medical and natural historical books attributed to her; though the proceedings to have her canonized as a saint in 1233 praise her medical skills and her medical books; and though medieval admirers such as the 13th-century Matthew of Westminster ascribed those texts to her, yet a late Victorian critic has insisted that Hildegard of Bingen was not the medical writer she had been thought to be. On the basis of his perverse judgment Dr. Hildegard of Bingen has been banished from most analyses of medieval medical practice.

The allegations of Hildegard of Bingen's medical non-existence are perplexing. As with Trotula, more so with Hildegard of Bingen: in her own time her genuineness and her medical effectiveness were unquestioned.

Hildegard's two medical texts are *Subtleties of Natural Creations* and *Cases and Cures*. Both contain intriguing theories of man and woman's nature, particularly the relationship between human physiology and the total universal order. Hildegard offers eminently practical medical and surgical techniques for most diseases of the body. She recommends treatments for a range of ailments, from skin diseases and simple fractures to epilepsy and madness. She suggests medicinal mood changers (to overcome melancholy or excessive joy), amulets, and such jewels as jasper for comforting women in childbirth, and other gems, tucked in the cheek, for aiding fasting and weight control.

Hildegard recommends natural stimulants and depressants, antidotes to poisons, aphrodisiacs, anti-aphrodisiacs, and appreciation of animals, birds, plants, and minerals which affect health. A superb analyst of human emotion, Hildegard stresses that for some cures it is not an inherent virtue in the medication or even its occult significance. If the patient believes the method will work, it will work. Modern scientists are still intrigued by the power of the placebo effect.

Hildegard condemned astrology and magic while herself practicing various forms of augury, prognostication, and prediction. Like other 12th-century theorists, she maintained that the human being is a microcosm, the total created universe writ small. At the beginning of *Cases and Cures* she compliments both God and humanity: "Consider the human being. In the body are the heavens and the earth, and all things are latent. For all things there are correspondences. The heavenly firmament to the human head, the moon and stars to the eyes, the air to hearing, winds to smelling, dew to taste, the sides of the world to the arms."

Elsewhere, delighting in the human and celestial numbers seven and three, she maintains that perfect proportions of the human body are comparable to those in the heavens. From the top of the cerebral cavity to the "last extremity of the forehead" are seven distinct equal spaces comparable to the seven major equidistant planets. The body was believed to be governed by a rule of three: just as there are three equal human distances between the top of the head and throat, throat to navel, navel to groin, so are the spaces equal intervening between the highest firmament, lowest clouds, the earth's surface and its center. Corresponding to these intervals are the ages of man: infancy, adolescence, and old age.

Though human and divine structures were considered perfect in relationship, Dr. Hildegard of Bingen believed that human beings dare not consult the stars for horoscope. The Sun, Moon, and stars are signs to human beings only by God's permission. Stars show signs of the future only by mirroring human acts. "The air receives an impression of something already revealed to human thought, which impression the stars reflect back to other people if God allows it." Condemning astrology, while yet attracted by it because she fervently believed that God's works are demonstrable in all aspects of His creation, Hildegard of Bingen's arguments were predictive of the theories of the Jewish philosopher-physician Maimonides, who lived and wrote 50 years after her.

The four humors of the body, the body's essential fluids—blood, phlegm, black bile, and yellow bile—ebb and flow in disequilibrium during sickness. High blood pressure makes blood rage like the rapid "leopard" pulse. Other states and diseases make the humors move sluggishly like the crab. Emotions, fevers, diseases, and injuries cause the pulse, monitoring the blood, and the other fluid sensors to states comparable to actions of wolf, bear, serpent, or lamb. Variations in the human pulse have diagnostic and prognostic importance. All creation is divinely interrelated.

Logic, according to Hildegard of Bingen, requires planning of all human acts, including sexual intercourse. If the Moon is life's most important orb, making certain days favorable for certain acts and others particularly malevolent, and men and women are clever enough to not sow crops in either midsummer or mid-winter, it is a pity that people foolishly beget children attending to pleasure and not to propitious times. This causes birth defects.

Born on a certain day at a particular hour, a child takes on the character of the celestial sign: choleric, sanguine, melancholy, or phlegmatic, and the attendant physique, personality, predilections, and professions. Physicians and clockmakers are born beneath the sign of Mercury; poets, cooks and aesthetes under Venus.

Not the planets themselves but the effects of these planets upon the air in turn affect the blood and humors of the body. Dr. Hildegard of Bingen, a daughter of her time, maintains pagan astrological ideas, subsuming them to Christian order. Ever the pragmatic physician, Hildegard insists that certain medications and surgical procedures will work at some times and not at others. The fault is not in the medical technique nor the practitioner but in the stars. The hands of healing are bound by astrological time.

Medieval European medical women, licensed and unlicensed, ministering to both male and female patients at all critical moments of life, practiced medicine and surgery vigorously, commandingly, productively, successfully. Physicians and surgeons, pharmacologists and pharmacists, health officers and trauma medics worked in war and in peace with knowledge, daring, technical skill, and practical savvy. The hands of many spectacular medieval women at work were hands of healing.

LADY BOSSES:
RULERS OF MANORS
AND MONASTERIES

Queen Eleanor of Aquitaine was born to command. She commanded well. Four kings she either bedded or birthed. Consort and coruler with two kings, she was kingmaker to two more, her sons Richard and John. Since modesty is hypocrisy, she chose never to be the hypocrite. Knowing her worth, she acknowledged few women or men as more powerful or more learned than herself, except that wonder of learned power, the Virgin Queen, who chose the King of all Kings to be her son.

To celebrate that matchless maiden, the Virgin Mary, but equally to share the grand adventure, she accompanied her first husband, King Louis VII of France on Crusade. Hearing St. Bernard preach, she only guessed the rigors of the Crusade road and the terrible glories of war for peace.

When she was very young, her father's court in Aquitaine attracted the most vibrant thinkers, artists, poets, singers, dancers, and tutors to speak, to perform, and to teach. Women were trained to erudite passion. They arbitrated taste in art, literature, and philosophy.

She became queen at 15. Marrying King Louis, she regretted leaving the glorious southern culture in Aquitaine. She lived in Paris with Louis, a dullish, monkish man. When she reached 30, her marriage was annulled.

A well-dowered woman did not long remain alone. She married Louis's rival, Henry, rigorous, vigorous duke of Normandy, soon to be king of England. To their court in London, she invited poets, performers, clerics, cooks, and courtiers who brought the best of southern French civilization to strong Anglo-Saxon ideas. Bernart de Ventadorn came to her court, praising her fame, singing elegantly of ecstatic love pain.

Her son Richard the Lion-Heart was as skilled a poet as he was powerful a warrior. Imprisoned in the Austrian castle of Durnstein, he wrote songs voicing fury in captivity.

Music, literature, and art exhilarated her while she worked with Henry shaping kingdoms. By law, by battle, and by court intrigue, they built mightily. She purchased property, devotion, churches, and the power of her sons against their father when Henry betrayed her.

Her astrologer reported that she would live till age 82. She did. She rested her final sleep at the abbey she had handsomely endowed at Fontevrault. In years to come, women and men there hailed both Mary and Eleanor.

While more dazzling and more powerful than most medieval women leaders, Queen Eleanor was a member of a venerable tradition of dominant women who were co-rulers with their husbands, regents for their young sons, surrogates for their husbands away at war or on crusade, widows of dead lords whose lands they ruled, or commanders of their own vast inheritances.

To be vested with enormous authority is a fine thing. But, as Mark Twain said, to have the onlooking world consent to it is even finer. Eleanor of Aquitaine had both authority and consent. Likewise, other dominant women between the 11th and 16th centuries successfully ran their countries, states, or households.

DIRECTING THE HOUSEHOLD

Running the medieval household was comparable to directing a small town. The lady boss was responsible for the huge supplies necessary for the care, feeding, and daily living of hundreds, sometimes thousands of people. Superintending the kitchen meant not only guiding food preparation for courtiers, servants, and workers, but controlling farms, forests, hunting preserves, fishing lakes, and herb gardens that provided the raw materials. The bakeries, wine cellars, larders, pantries, and spiceries were under her jurisdiction, as were the farm laborers, hunters, cooks, bakers, carvers, kitchen help, banquet servitors, musicians, dancers, and jugglers.

Clothing and fabric making for the whole household usually was the women's responsibility, from sheep-shearing to spinning, from weaving to tailoring. Superintending the house meant guiding all the workers on the buildings and grounds: maids, grooms, masons, painters, plasterers, roofers, plumbers, carpenters, chimney sweeps, gardeners, arborists, stable hands, carters, drivers, falconers, and security personnel for the main castle or manor house plus its auxiliary buildings.

Hiring, firing, paying, directing, adjudicating, the lady boss supervised not only kitchen and hall but the education of her children, and sometimes the education of all children on the manor, obtaining their tutors, chamberlains, scribes, and chaplains.

Whether ruling alone or with her husband, she usually had responsibility for the court's cultural life, selecting poets, propagandists, manuscript makers, scribes, illuminators, sculptors, artisans, troubadours, jongleurs, and other people paid to decorate by their art the chapel and hall. Though not necessarily permanent members of the household, nevertheless during their tenure of months or years, the lady usually was their patron.

For all her staff, the medieval woman leader was the quasi-legal arbitrator of disputes, often holding court, handing down judgments, and assigning punishments. She was also the quasi-official health officer responsible for their care in illness. Literally laying on the hands of healing, the lady boss was well-trained in practical medicine, expected to be facile in diagnosis and treatment.

Moreover, she was responsible for security of her domain. Women successfully held their castles against attack, vigorously protecting their property and people from assault.

While not every medieval woman leader had all these responsibilities, many had most. Legal records, account books, household payment ledgers, instruction books such as those of Christine de Pizan, and personal letters such as Margaret Paston's demonstrate medieval women's leadership responsibilities.

Opposite: Elegantly clothed and seated at the high table, the hostess, beneath a richly decorated baldachin canopy, greets the entertainers who regale the guests with music and mummery. Sword-carrying musicians play a variety of fifes, flutes, recorders, shawms, drums, and stringed instruments. Bird-masked, armed entertainers mime and act a play. Most mumming preserved ancient fertility rites including beheadings and resurrections, as in Morris Dances. The lead mummer carries a baton or torch, and faces the ermine-collared Surveyor of Ceremonies who directs the feast, alternating courses with entertainments.

Responsible leadership is an extreme form of servitude. The work schedule for the medieval lady boss was formidable. She was obliged to publicly express qualities of command: organization, vigor, diplomacy, and daring good sense. A typical day in the life of a lady boss can be created from such an instruction book for women in power as Christine de Pizan's *Book of the Three Virtues.* Christine de Pizan describes the lady exercising her responsibility predawn to midnight. Ladies of lesser political power but nevertheless great wealth and responsibility had comparable labors.

After a few hours for sleep, the lady boss would awaken before dawn. She would dress and eat breakfast before attending chapel, which was as much a political as a religious responsibility. The lady ruler was not obliged to spend as much time in lengthy prayers as those who had greater leisure, for the ruler derived much merit for attending to the public good and the welfare of those in her power.

Leaving the chapel, she had to give alms and listen to requests from poor petitioners, granting promptly and generously whatever she might, not only for charity, but also to enhance her reputation. If unable to hear all the beggings, she had to delegate the job to an honorable, efficient surrogate. The Lady was responsible for his actions.

If her government council met in the morning, she had to conduct herself with such bearing and countenance that seated on the high seat of authority she not only governed well but created the impression of doing so. Enormous authority requires acknowledgment by the ruled. To be revered as wise, masterful, and powerful, she had to listen diligently to all proposals and opinions, weighing carefully the best advice. She had to

reply cogently and sagely. If possible she would have had advance briefings by her counselors on all important matters.

Thereafter she had to preside at a noon-time feast. People were seated according to social protocol, and served foods varying in type and quantity according to their rank. Entertainments in the hall included dramatic readings of poems of ancient deeds, or music or plays both edifying and delightful. As the feasting ended, the lady boss held audience for those who came from afar to seek her counsel or her money. Receiving each graciously with due honor, she spoke seriously to the elderly, and to the young more gaily.

After sharing digestive spices to adjourn the feast, she moved to her private apartment for a brief rest. There she did useful handwork such as embroidery or weaving. She shared simple talk and amusement with her ladies-in-waiting. Politics here was as important as friendship. The lady boss's laughter and informal talk encouraged her women to faithfulness and discretion, so that they would "love her with great devotion." She also learned the latest court news.

Next she visited the sick, in hospitals, or, if they were members of her own household (gentlemen, stewards, or farmers), in their quarters, touching with her hands of healing.

Then she did the financial books. A medieval lady maintained five classes of expense accounts, appropriately distributing her income. First was for gifts to the poor. Second was the money for her household: hundreds of men and women fed and paid from her own revenues, the taxes

Noble men and women hunters usually brought the catch to the kitchen as trophy, but essentially hunted not for food but for exercise, joy in the sport, and entertainment. Hunting instruction books, often magnificently illustrated, written by Gaston Phebus, King Frederick of Sicily, and others, depicted the ceremony and sport, and methods of tracking, chasing, killing, and carving prey. Hunt manuals usually contain advice on animal husbandry and on medical uses of animal parts to treat and cure disease and injury. Falconry, or hawking, was a technique for hunting game with birds of prey such as falcons and other hawks. Birds were trained to the wrist and hoodwinked (temporarily blinded by hoods over their heads to prevent jitters), held, as this woman hunter holds her hawk, by long leather thongs called jesses, and then let fly to musical calls. King Frederick II's famous falconry text, Tractatus de arte venandi cum avibus (The art of hunting with birds), and other hunt manuals were imitated by writers of love allegories, who used the language of the chase for depicting the arts of courtly love. Medieval poems and songs such as the chasse, caccia, and catch express human passion with the rhythms and rhetoric of the hunt. Troubadour, trouvère, and minnesinger songs as well as fabliaux exploit connections between hunting and love. Such poems appear in one of the more magnificent illustrated songbooks from the 13th and 14th centuries, the Manesse Manuscript of Songs of the Minnesingers, which includes 6,000 songs of 140 poets with 137 full-page gold and polychrome miniatures, such as this elegant page.

and rents paid directly to her. The third account paid her officers and court ladies, counselors, and ambassadors to distant holdings or foreign courts. A fourth account was reserved for gifts to strangers or to her subjects who evidenced particular merit. Such patronage allowed the lady boss to encourage art, science, and technology within her domain, and to be celebrated for generosity. A final personal treasury was for purchasing her own jewels, gowns, and apparel.

This same afternoon, she had to visit her children. Children were not only a maternal exercise but a political requirement. Carefully having arranged their proper tutoring, the lady boss who was a mother had to consistently guide their activities, intermittently checking on their progress. As Christine says, "the greatest protection and ornament she can have is her children, for as often happens someone who might wish to harm the mother will refrain from doing so for fear of the children." Eleanor of Aquitaine raised her sons and daughters to learning as well as to her own protection. They went to war against their father King Henry II to advance their mother's cause.

In late afternoon she also might ride horseback, hunt, boat on the river, dance, or play chess, backgammon, or billiards. All public entertainments served policy. Certainly the lady boss was not to allow herself to be checkmated.

Sometimes before supper on an active day she would supervise purchase of foodstuffs from merchants, for the imported delicacies, spices, and herbs. Maintaining good relationships with merchants by paying promptly for goods and services, she kept her credit respectable. She was also obligated to supervise the cook's menus, providing great varieties and quantities of food for all classes eating within the great hall, and was responsible for tasting the wines and ales whose quality made the political assertion: my power bought this.

When the sun set toward Vespers' time, the lady boss would say evening prayers in chapel or chamber, before exercising in the garden in advance of supper. She would not wander alone, for she had to hold a late afternoon audience with her subjects who needed her. She may, according to Christine, have had to indulge in discreet dissimulation with her enemies lest she appear to be in any way weakening her control over people or purses. This twilight stroll was as political as it was healthful.

Supper, again a public meal, had entertainments. Many were political. Reading histories aloud or chanting dramatic stories that glorified the court or the Lady reaffirmed her control over the listeners and their lives.

After this evening banquet, the lady boss went to her prayers and her bed. Extraordinarily busy dawn-light through candlelight with activities that were far from boring or merely ceremonial, the responsible lady boss only briefly slept. Her vocation required physical stamina as well as exemplary control over emotions and actions. Scrutinized by a public either wishing her well or desiring her dead, the medieval lady boss constantly arranged events so that her power was acknowledged and reaffirmed.

Numerous 12th- through 15th-century women leaders similarly labored under rigorous schedules. To customary responsibilities the lady boss intermittently added riding off to crusade; arduous voyages visiting landholdings; political travels to new acquisitions got by diplomacy or war; visits to markets, fairs, and banking houses; and the defense of her establishments by the sword.

Numerous women swore to guard their properties with their lives— and succeeded. Fifteenth-century English Margaret Paston, for example, while her husband was journeying on business, found enemies attacking their manor. She valiantly defended it while the bombarded walls crumbled and her household retainers fell dead at her feet. She reports this in a letter to her husband recounting it as a usual occurrence consistent with other duties of a woman at work.

On the northerly borders of England, women guarded their domains. The 14th-century Scottish countess of Buchan defended Burwick Castle against attack by King Edward I. The king later hung the countess in a cage from the ramparts of Burwick as punishment for her temerity.

Lady Alice Knyvet in 1461 refused to give up Bokenham Castle to the king, who had ordered 10 commissioners and a justice of the peace to claim it on the spot by legal proceedings. When they arrived, they discovered the drawbridge up and Alice and her 50 men armed with swords, glaives, and bows and arrows. The Patent Rolls in the London archives report Alice shouting from a tower, "Mister Twyer, you are a justice of the peace. I require you to keep the peace. I will not leave possession of this castle. If you make war to take this place from me, I shall defend myself. I prefer in such wise to die. My husband and my honor charge me to keep this place." She kept it.

Opposite: Wearing a sumptuously brocaded robe with huge, pendent sleeves lined with ermine, and a headdress that partially covers her lavishly braided hair, a noblewoman presents her children to their royal grandfather. Crowned and seated on a throne beneath a fringed baldachin upheld by stout columns, the monarch greets his family while his counselor gesticulates at his side. Children's costumes emulated adults' clothes. Sumptuary laws regulated by profession or class who could wear which fabric, fur, color, or style.

ARRANGED MARRIAGE

Many pledges of faithfulness to a spouse were made by youngsters. The typical lady boss gained her position through an arranged marriage. Marriage by choice for love is a relatively modern indulgence. (Given modern divorce rates, apparently it is not a more successful institution than medieval marriage by arrangement.) While medieval marriage customs varied according to country or century, nevertheless marriage essentially was the parents' affair. Particularly among the noble, landed, and rich, *children* married, as children.

Parents often arranged their children's marriages before any likelihood of physical readiness. Medieval noble husbands and wives often played ball, hoops, read Latin, and danced together before puberty allowed consummation of their union. Seven-year-old brides were common. Betrothing their children to unite large land holdings or resolve disputes between warring families, parents made nuptial pledges for purely dynastic purposes.

One dared not spend too long on childhood in an age before antibacterial drugs and antibiotics made common infections no longer lethal, when the average age at death was no older than 33. Once reaching puberty or the usual age of consent to marriage, which was 14 for boys and 12 for girls, young spouses in arranged marriages could request annulment if either did not willingly consent to the union. Though Gracian, the great churchman and canon lawyer, insisted that a married youngster's consent was necessary, families created ways to secure unwilling unions.

Thinking she could compel her daughter via an offer she could not refuse, Margaret Paston locked up her recalcitrant girl in a tower, permitting neither visitors nor food, until she would consent to marry an

old, rich man of her mother's choice. The young lady, slimmer and stubborner for her ordeal, ultimately triumphed with the young lover of her own choice.

With child marriage the rule, infant engagement was common. A 14th-century English document seals the engagement of two noble children still *in utero*. A nobleman consecrated as husband the unborn son in the womb of his pregnant wife to the other nobleman's as yet unborn daughter. A safety clause allowed for reversal of sexes, or abrogation of the agreement if both babes were born of the same sex.

The family of Euginia Picot poignantly exemplifies child marriage. Associated with the court of King Henry and Queen Eleanor in England, Euginia was the daughter of Ralf Picot, from whom she inherited lands in Wilton, Kent. Aged 30, she had been married and widowed twice.

Opposite: At her bridal feast, the slender bride, seated regally beneath a red canopied baldachin, allows her long golden hair to cascade down her back, cinched above by her elaborate gold and red headdress called a crowned atour. *Her hat's two "horns" are stylistically related to the single-horn hats, or* hennins, *fashionable in 15th-century Europe, that her two gentlewomen wear. With pendent, diaphanous veils called* lambrequins, *hennins enabled a small woman to appear tall and a noblewoman effectively to assert power. Her hat usually was the tallest spire in a procession, emulating the Gothic cathedral's vault and vertical skywards thrust toward God in Heaven. A carver serves the women at the high table whole birds. Servants enter the dining hall from the kitchen to serve guests seated at the long table, the* sideboard. *Musicians standing in an overhead gallery play fanfares on long trumpets to announce the progression of courses in the feast, to entertain, and to aid digestion. A blue-robed Surveyor of Ceremonies presides over the feast service, standing near a tall Gothic wooden* aumbry *displaying silver and gold pitchers and platters. A white-pawed hound majestically prances on the decorated tile floor. The servitors, shod in long-pointed* poulaines, *wear cinch-waisted buttock-hugging tunics called* pourpoints *whose extravagantly exaggerated shoulders and sleeves are extended by cylindrical pads called* mahoîtres. *Fifteenth-century noble costume complemented the exquisite physiques both women and men cultivated by exercise and diet.*

Euginia's first husband was William Malet, a member of the royal household, who died in 1170, leaving Euginia an inheritance in Cambridgeshire. Subsequently married to Thomas Fitz Bernard, chief forester for the king and queen, Euginia Picot produced one daughter and three sons, who in 1185, at their father's death, were aged 10, eight, and three.

King Henry had given Euginia's daughter, named Maude, in marriage to an infant boy, the heir of John de Bidun. However, the baby-boy groom died. Young Maude was a widow at age 10. She lived in custody of her mother, who controlled her marriage-inherited lands. Mother Euginia, however, held yet another child's dowry. Her eldest son at age 10 already was married, to a five-year old heiress who had brought her land, a large Essex manor, with her.

By complex laws of feudal prerogatives and responsibilities, King Henry had the right to give widow Euginia's daughter in marriage. Inheritance law, widowhood, wardship, and feudal incidents all affected women's estates. In various countries daughters were their parents' prime heirs. In some cases women were co-heirs with other male or female siblings. Some estates consisted of gigantic lands, farms, manors, and incomes as well as such moveable property as jewelry or gold. Inheritance laws in the same country frequently varied from district to district.

Inheriting fortunes empowered women. It also endangered freedom. Law, the feudal overlord, or the king required that certain valuable properties be disposable only by themselves. A wealthy widow's remarriage became an affair of state. Certain widows were said to be "in the king's hand," requiring his formal permission to marry again. Naturally, it was in the king's interest to assure a good male courtier or valiant knight in allegiance to himself through the marriage with a widow under his jurisdiction. With the woman's land came such feudal incidents as the knight's military service to the ruler.

Marital matches acceptable to the king or overlord were choices more dynastic than ardent. But the estates involved could be large or minuscule. Listings of women's worth from rural Rutland, England, suggest that not only the richest noblewomen required consent to remarry.

Roheis de Bussey was "gift of the lord king." Her land in Essendine was worth ten pounds along with the stock of three plows and one hundred sheep. The sheep were missing. Roheis was 60 years old and had two daughters as heirs, both married.

Alice de Beaufow, widow of Thomas, was in the "gift of the lord king." She was 20 years old and had a two-year-old son, her heir. Her valuable land in Seton possessed the following stock: two plows, one hundred sheep, two draft animals, five sows, one boar, and four cows. Her recently received rents for her land included 36s. 10d., 2 pounds of pepper, gifts from her tenants valued at 4s., and 3 loads of oats.

These documents also remind us that daughters inherited from mothers, just as sons inherited money and title from their mothers as well as their fathers.

Medieval women "in the king's hand" or "gift of the lord king" were not being sold or treated as mere chattel, available for acquisition or disposition according to an overlord's desire. They had some freedom to choose: they often could buy their way out of adherence to the overlord's decision through payment of money or service. Moreover, it was generally recognized that the overlord or king had valid political reasons for requiring his consent for a widow's marriage, and that he was doing a good deed in taking care of the widow and ward. In modern context such care seems like condescending paternalism. In the Middle Ages it was the overlord or king's duty, and often his legal responsibility, to protect widows and children.

Feudal overlords were legally required to protect their subjects' safety. The functions of police and army were filled by the service of each pledged knight and his retinue. The overlord selecting or approving of a powerful widow's new husband shielded himself against an ineffectual or treasonous knight in his service. A danger at war and a financial inconvenience at peace, an uncooperative new husband for a rich landed widow might compromise not only the king's person or his income but also his ability to carry out his obligations.

Patronage was yet another value of a widow's choice being held in her overlord's hand. A good woman's hand and her good land were a potent reward to a faithful male courtier. The possibility of such a reward was a significant lure to a courtier's patriotic fealty.

For all these reasons, a king or overlord often required documentation of a woman's intention to abide by his will. Fourteenth-century English archives preserve numerous such agreements. Hawisia, widow of William de la Pluenke, was given a dower which she would receive when she promised not to marry without King Edward III's consent. Queen Philippa had ultimate custody of the land until the young heir of Hawisia and William came of age. Likewise, Juliana, widow of William de

Paunton, was given a "reasonable dower" after she swore under oath not to marry without the king's consent. So also Margaret, widow of Thomas Graunson, promised to not marry without the king's license; the king created her dower from lands she inherited from her husband.

At the death of her husband, Sir Edward, in 1376, Elizabeth le Despenser inherited formidable properties and incomes from castles, forests, and rental properties. She swore homage and fealty to King Edward III and promised him her service as a knight. She pledged not to marry without the king's license. Thereupon the king returned "her right and heritage" of properties both in England and on the border of Wales: castles, towns, churches, abbeys, and priories.

Some medieval women leaders may have been flighty, flirtatious, and philandering. But the responsibilities of lady bosses required long, hard days of work extending into night. Most lady bosses also labored at night as their husbands' bed partners and providers of their heirs.

DIRECTING CHURCH FACILITIES

Lady bosses of the church had similar responsibilities to women leaders in castle and town. Abbesses and prioresses who ruled nunneries and monasteries were responsible for the political and practical wellbeing of thousands. At the French monastic community Fontevrault, in whose abbey Queen Eleanor of Aquitaine was buried, the abbess ruled nearly 10,000 men and women.

Controlling most of the same functions as the secular woman leader, the medieval church woman in power also guarded for her community and their parishioners the liturgies of prayer, and, theoretically, the people's immortal souls.

Small and large nunneries had enormous wealth. Others lived in patient poverty, dedicated to contemplation and prayer. Women mystics such as Marjorie Kempe and Julian of Norwich had their followers. Fontevrault and similar houses funded with royal money were as lavish as secular courts. Their full stories are not yet known. What truly was the power of women's movements such as the Beguines, the Poor Clares, and the Cistercian nuns? What truly were the rights and responsibilities of the lady bosses who ran the double monasteries, the coeducational religious houses joining monks and nuns? How did some nuns avoid the jurisdiction of the male hierarchy of the church? How did powerful women's religious movements in the Middle Ages function exempt from the authority of bishops?

Themselves often noble, educated, monied, and astute, these nuns wielded powers beyond the bounds of the cloister. Many a talented nun or abbess was the daughter of a nobleman who could not raise an adequate dowry for her. Daughters, widows, and wives desiring escape from an unfavorable marriage became the competent ecclesiastical leaders of nunneries and the abbess-leaders ruling coeducational monastic communities uniting the works and days of monks with nuns.

Abbesses of abbeys for nuns and leaders of double monasteries for monks and nuns managed vast lands and finances, collecting taxes and tithes, directing scholarly projects, organizing *scriptoria* for copying manuscripts, arbitrating disputes on associated farms and town lands, arguing differences with rival churchmen or the pope himself, establishing hospitals and clinics, and judging ecclesiastical questions of liturgy and miracle. Consecrating the men and women religious to the work of God, churchwomen built churches, hired priests, and directed care and repair of their buildings.

Lady bosses in the church superintended farms and forests, bought property, and built houses, barns, and churches. Like secular noble women, the abbesses collected rents, negotiated financial deals, hired and fired men and women laborers, traveled to distant land holdings, made pilgrimages to local shrines and to Jerusalem, adjudicated disputes among community dissidents, and fought incursions against their government.

Dominant churchwomen added to these responsibilities others associated with money. Some apparently even minted their own. By legal maneuvering, and by such extralegal techniques as forging documents, the medieval woman church leader protected the interests of her house against greedy noblemen or kings desiring to collect rent or homage, and against voracious churchmen.

The Anglo-Saxon abbess Hilda, for example, of the coeducational monastery at Whitby, had a miracle on her hands—or an ignorant shepherd's fraud. Her word determined which. Shy, illiterate, stuttering Caedmon began to compose glorious words and verses. He became so renowned a wordsmith that he was called England's first poet. The Venerable Bede relates how Abbess Hilda judged that his new talent was a miraculous manifestation of God's will.

No mere intellectual exercise, a decision on miracles had financial as well as political effects. A true miracle not only assured status for her house but a lucrative pilgrimage trade to fill her community's coffers as the faithful flocked to the holy shrine. The abbess became keeper of the faith's coin.

As a practical hard-laboring administrator, the abbess oftentimes was patron of both medicine and learning. A famous, learned, medically adept leader of church women was Héloïse of Argenteuil and Paraclete. Popularly remembered for her passionate love affair with the scholar-theologian Abelard, Héloïse achieved her position as an ecclesiastical leader after their secret marriage was discovered. She was banished to a convent. Abelard was brutally castrated. While scandal assured her modern fame, talent enabled her to triumph as a learned nun, like Abbess Hilda of Whitby and Hersende of Fontevrault, vested with enormous authority and mightily wielding it against kings and bishops.

Many an abbess can even be said to have been a *de facto* bishop. Women's abbeys and coeducational monasteries often were exempt from paying taxes to noblemen and kings and freed of providing service to them. Certain women's communities did not pay the church tithes otherwise due to the bishop. The abbess and her community were exempt from the bishop's authority. So also were the secular clergy serving them and the laity within the village churches belonging to the monasteries. All were directly dependent upon the Holy See in Rome. The effect of such exemptions was to give the abbess a position of quasi-episcopal jurisdiction.

Such an abbess had the same duties and rights to act within her separate territories as a bishop had within his diocese. Rights of jurisdiction enabled the abbess herself to collect all tithes, rents, and monies due to the church. She had all ecclesiastical and civil administration under her control. In her territory, the abbess's spiritual and temporal jurisdiction was phrased in canon law *nullius diocesis* or *praelatura nullius,* subservient to no diocese and no prelate.

The abbess was ordained. She heard confession. The spiritual mother as confessor could impose penance and grant absolution for sin. Such a cleric was called the holiest or most powerful holy woman, or *sacerdos maxima.*

Medieval men bishops did not appreciate this tradition of female independence, traceable back to words of Christ Himself. Throughout the Middle Ages various bishops railed against independent churchwomen. Bishops insisted upon their right to investigate women's monastic houses, and to collect their monies and valuables. However, certain churchwomen maintained their independence right up to the 15th-century Council of Trent.

Queens helped women's abbeys, and abbesses catered to queens. The Fontevrault order started in France with branch houses throughout Europe, with particularly powerful houses in England; it thrived longer in independence than most other abbeys. Numerous papal bulls renewed prohibitions against archbishops, deacons, and all ecclesiastical people from taking over nuns' churches or excommunicating them. The pope sometimes merely restated the local king's orders. King Henry II, for example, had granted liberties for the Fontevrault nuns. The ecclesiastical and secular documents are worded almost identically. Queen Eleanor of Aquitaine, as an enthusiastic and generous benefactor of Fontevrault, may have been the beneficent genius behind these churchwomen's rights.

It must be emphasized that these rights were not mere theoretical vestings of authority. The Prioress of Clerkenwell near London controlled her community's property ranging over 11 counties around London and 64 parish churches within London. The abbess ruled over monks' houses as well as the nuns'. She supervised the churches. She collected tithes. She built and maintained church buildings. She provided salaries for her priests. She influenced their sermons.

A typical day in the life of an ecclesiastical woman leader resembled remarkably that of her secular colleague. For the religious, however, three elements differed. Prayer was preeminent, if not in practice then certainly by proposition. Prescriptions for prayer and proscriptions against activities deflecting from prayer enabled the nun-prioress to observe seven of the eight canonical hours for prayer: rising early, before dawn, for Matins, then ranging at three hour intervals through Prime, Terce, Sext, Nones, Vespers, Compline, and Lauds.

In the divine service, the medieval lady leader celebrated not only Christ but more so his marvelous mother, Matchless Mary, Virgin progenetrix. Particularly in Eleanor of Aquitaine's holdings in the south of France and in England, praise of Mary, Mariology, developed into such extravagant emphasis upon mother over child that it became a nearly heretical enthusiasm called Mariolatry. Queens and abbesses, as noble, learned, imperially powerful lady bosses, eulogized in religion their *alma mater*. The medieval prioress, the mother superior, if herself not physically a virgin, often was a noble mother retiring from ruling the court in favor of directing the nunnery. Even if she had borne children, she became a newly consecrated "virgin to God."

After prayer, the abbess engaged in a second activity different from the pursuits of her secular counterpart: learning and manuscript copying. While queens such as Eleanor of Aquitaine were patrons for the writing of glorious books, various monastic houses had *scriptoria,* actual writing factories for creating manuscripts. Nuns as scribes were famous for their exquisite writing techniques, producing prodigious numbers of pages and works.

Hroswitha of Gandersheim was famous as scribe, playwright, and poet. Other nuns were important manuscript illuminators, rubricators, marginalia makers, and painters of notable illustrations. Convents such as St. Catherine's at St. Gall's were particularly famous for their manuscripts. Particular nun calligraphers were in great demand, such as the indefatigable Diemude of the monastery of Wessobrun, who in the 11th century produced thousands of pages by her hand: missals, bibles, epistles, histories, saints' lives, gospels, and philosophical works, a veritable public library.

The third major characteristic distinguishing the ecclesiastical lady boss was her professional expertise in medicine. Abbess Hildegard of Bingen, for instance, was a physician so extraordinary her cures were considered miracles and she herself a saint. Another famous and successful medical woman of the 12th century was Abbess Harrad of Landsberg. Running a medical clinic with 47 nun assistants, Harrad welcomed patients coming great distances for her remarkable healing powers. No mere faith healer, she practiced intelligently according to the best scientific ideas of the 12th century. Like Hildegard of Bingen, Harrad of Landsberg derived most of her medical and surgical techniques from the writings of such notable women practitioner-theorists as Dr. Trotula of Salerno. Harrad calligraphed and illustrated her own encyclopedia. Her *Hortus Deliciarum* (Garden of delights), was a book of knowledge for her nuns. Her encyclopedia united medical ideas with theories of cosmology.

Most other daily chores of the woman church leader startlingly paralleled the secular. Meals were social events, bringing nuns together in pious reverence for God's gifts. For edification more than entertainment, a reader or singer might chant stories during meals.

Noble nuns also carried secular tastes into the cloister dining room. As visiting bishop Eudes of Rouen noted while investigating the convent of Montvilliers, numerous frivolities deflected thought to pleasure. Nuns sat gossiping in social cliques, eating exotic foods according to their social rank, delighting in dishes beyond the *pittances,* those small extra food gifts allowed on holidays or for good behavior. They utilized fancy tableware. In the refectory they had entertainers performing for them recklessly risqué songs, dances, and dramatic interludes.

Bishop Eudes visited that convent neither by invitation nor by rule, recording in his report the angry protestation from the abbess. She insisted that her cloister was exempt from his jurisdiction. She challenged his right to criticize and to condemn the fashionable, pleasurable activities in their sacred halls.

Sharing credit for excellence but personally and solely taking blame for failure, the ruler rules by lonely, hard work. Authority requires passion to wield it well. Medieval women granted prestige had their power acknowledged by friends and foes. Medieval lady bosses epitomized power's perilous pleasure and pleasurable peril.

4

CRAFTSWOMEN: IN MARKETS, FIELDS, AND MINES

anguage gives us wonderful clues to the social order of the past—if only we know where to look. At a recent conference, I was delighted to note how many family names on the list of presenters reflected the work of craftswomen.

Dr. Kaufman's ancestor was a merchant. Dr. Chandler's was a candle-maker. Dr. Cooper's forbear was a beer-barrel-maker. Dr. Schneider's family name came from a clothcutter or tailor, and another was named after a Hungarian version of "tailor," Szabo. While my list had a Dr. Baker, representing the male breadmaker, there was a Dr. Baxter, reflecting the heritage of a professional woman baker (the medieval word *baker*, approximately pronounced bokker, plus its feminine ending made *bakesterre*, which became *baxter*). Webster represents the crafts*woman*'s heritage in the cloth trades. The crafts*man*'s family name would be Weaver or Webber. Dr. Brewster's ultimate progenatrix was a brewer of beer or ale. If his origin traced back to a male craftsman, his name would have been Brewer. Dr. Lavender preserved the heritage of the important medieval craft of laundering cloth: cleaning, finishing, and "sizing" wools and silks. A professional cloth-washer-man was called a Laver.

My list glittered with matronymics, family names inherited through a mother's heritage. Soon my list divided, like a cell in mitosis, my mother list becoming two daughter lists, one of family names representing professional women in the food crafts, the other women in the cloth trade. In a footnote to my clothier list I added two other modern words traceable to medieval craftswomen. While not family names nevertheless they indicate family position. Spinster, now the epithet for an unmarried woman, refers to the professional spinners of wool, silk, cotton, or linen thread used in clothmaking, weaving, and embroidery. Her tool called the distaff is now a metaphor for woman and also denotes her relatives, the distaff side of the family. All these cloth craft and food craft names accurately represent two major classes of medieval craftswomen's work in the fields, markets, and mines of Western Europe.

Medieval craftswomen were numerous and powerful. Various craft guilds had women members as well as Master-directors. Some guilds, such as the silk weavers in London in the 14th century, were exclusively female. Medieval girls and women were legally apprenticed to crafts with the same customary contractual obligations as for boys and men. Women craft experts themselves taught apprentices, both male and female.

Married women practicing their professions full time sometimes united vocation with family life. Other craftswomen kept their professional life separate. Special legal protection existed for the craftswoman, who under the law, either as a married woman worker or as an unmarried woman, could be a *femme sole,* a woman alone. The *femme sole* solely controlled her own income; her cash box was hers alone, free from acquisitive fingers of her relatives or husband. She solely was responsible for her debts and for her taxes. She solely was empowered to train apprentices.

Yet other mercantile rules protected women and their jobs against competition from local craftsmen and from foreign craftsmen. Silkwomen in London, for example, successfully petitioned the crown in 1368 against competition from Italian men silkworkers.

Specialties of medieval craftswomen ranged widely, with some of the wealthiest women earning their income from mercantile banking and wool exporting, such as 14th-century Rose of Burford, England, and commodity brokerage, such as the 12th-century women with whom Maimonides's brother David worked in Cairo, Egypt.

Subsistence craftswomen, farm wives augmenting family income by producing small quantities of bread or beer as a sideline job for pin money, are also discernible in town laws. Temporary jobs performed at home are called "bye" industries. Bye workers produced and sold directly to customers, usually neighbors or visitors to a fair.

Those who worked at home on items or parts that a retailer would later sell, such as an embroiderer of cape hems, a knitter of wool shirts, or a fabricator of iron bosses for jewel cases, were cottage workers, and their productions part of a cottage industry. An intermediary paid the cottage worker before integrating the product into the item sold to the customer. Bye work and cottage work were addressed in medieval market laws. More important legislation and litigation preserving medieval craftswomen's achievements pertain to those women who by vocation sold their talent, skill, labor, or products to the market. These businesswomen used what they had to get what they wanted. Trading value for value, they sold their time, their strength, and their wares for money.

A lucrative occupation for women and men was *regrating*. Regrators were retailers who bought goods and produce wholesale for resale at a profit, modest or large. Clever regrators could predict market fluctuations for particular commodities, or manipulate the market to artificially create shortages of a necessity and then provide it at high price. Grain regrators who bought low, held long, and sold high practiced the specialty called *afeering*.

Marriage and inheritance laws affected craftswomen of the field, market, and mines much as they affected the lives of noblewomen. Professions provided prestige and money. Business also provided an opportunity for social climbing, or a danger of exploitation. Penurious noblemen sought out monied women merchants and rich merchant widows. Money's pleasures enabled tradesmen's daughters to marry their way into the gentry. Rich merchant women, their exploits preserved in law documents and in fiction, manipulated their men by the purse strings. Rival merchant parents consolidated financial empires by the marriages of their children.

Women did not work in these crafts and businesses alone, exclusive of men, but they worked in these crafts and businesses just as men did. Women were professional cooks and weavers, just as men were. Women were paid for their work just as men were.

FABRIC TRADESWOMEN

Imagine an elaborate embroidered wool and silk-velvet cape and jewel-embellished hood. To create the raw materials for these exquisite garments women labored in sheepfolds, on silk farms, and in silver mines. Then women designed, sewed, wove, embroidered, and embellished the garments before other women sold them. Some women exported raw materials such as wool to an international market, and others imported precious jewels. The fabrication of the cape and hood shows women working at every level of the lucrative medieval cloth trades.

The cape is garnet-colored silk velvet, lined with a cotton twill. Front and back are exquisitely woven tapestried panels of finest wool with threads wound with spun gold and silver. The hood is blue silk velvet with seed pearls, semiprecious jewels set in metal bezels, and gold and silver embroidered borders. Craftswomen handled all of these elements, from cultivation of silkworms to silk to the final embellishments.

Every stage of the medieval European cloth trade in some country at some time was primarily in women's hands. The formidable wool trade in England created merchant family fortunes and dictated international alliances, from the shearing of sheep through the loading of wool bales onto ships, from the payments for raw wool through the complicated import-export duties. Women labored in the trade, sometimes dominated it, and occasionally monopolized aspects of it.

Sheep-shearing was a significant medieval vocation not only on family farms but on large acreage specifically dedicated to grazing. Special fleece scissors and cutters were used by the shearers who then baled their produce for market. So familiar was the woman sheep shearer, she became a figure of political satire: Jan Hus, the anti-Catholic reformer, satirizing the church's extortionate extractions of money from the poor, depicted holy church as a shearer fleecing her flock.

Once fleece reached market, spinsters spun it into thread or yarn. Thousands of women worked as spinners. Five spinsters on average kept one weaver working. Local cloth industries often imported yarn to keep looms shuttling. Probably the most common of women's *bye* industries, and reasonably lucrative, spinning was always in demand, and easily integrated with other routines. Spinning was an exclusively female profession.

More women cloth workers included kemsters who "combed" long filaments of wool or yarn; lavenders who washed, sized, and prevented shrinkage; nappers who raised the nap on deep pile fabrics; and listers or color dyers who colored yarn with exquisitely subtle variations, commonly using madder for red, weld for yellow, and woad for blue, plus other dyes in mineral mordants that allowed extraordinary range in wool hues. Ready for weaving, wool of various grades was classified, priced, and baled for sale to cloth makers and tapestry weavers.

Websters utilized techniques ranging from simple hand looms to complex frame and shuttle devices, either horizontal or vertical. The same techniques exist today. Automation increases the speeds of the original medieval technological designs, but not the excellence of production on the *basselisse* horizontal loom and the upright *hautelisse* looms still gracing tapestry factories in Arras and Paris.

For baling wool for export on ships, a women's guild in Southhampton, England, existed right into the 16th century, charged with packing the wool for loading and then stevedoring the loads onto ships. Two women were chosen annually as masters of their company, and all vacancies in their ranks were filled by nomination of the mayor and the corporation of Southhampton. Town regulations required the women to work "the balons and pokes with their own hands and to be sure not to scold one another."

Wealthy women wool merchants, such as Rose of Burford, were significant exporters. Yet other women held the high mercantile rank of "Merchant of the Staple," a position comparable today to the most revered life members of the stock exchange.

For the red silk velvet we must look to an even more exclusive women's craft: silk making. Women not only thrived in the trade but sometimes totally excluded men. From raising the silkworm cocoons, through fabrication of elegant silk belts and purses, women completely dominated the silk trade in several countries, their guild in France especially notable politically. Weaving silk into fabric or blending it with wool for tapestries and rugs, medieval women controlled a trade so lucrative that numerous lords and members of the gentry apprenticed their daughters to silkwomen, thus increasing the social status of silk making. Guild books for many towns record gentlewomen members as apprentices.

Since velvet has a high nap, special nappers would comb the surface with implements called nappers and teasles. Nappers were often women.

The making of cotton and linen cloth, needed for the lining of the cape, also was woman's work, from the picking of the raw material through the scutching of the flax to the actual weaving of the cloth. Towns were identified by the excellence of their women clothmakers.

R O - M A.

A L'Innentore che insegna come si debban met tere i bocciuoli per il seme.

B Gentildonna che accomoda i bocciuoli in vna scatola.

C Donzella che tien la scatola, & il coperchio di carta.

E Scatola, doue si pōgono i bocciuoli p far seme.

F Instrumento di carta forato da coprirla.

G Bragiero con vn poco di fuoco lento.

D Panno attaccato da alto in baffo, doue si lascia no star congiunte le farfalle.

O Il sole deue illuminar la stanza, mà non offen dere il panno co i raggi.

N Si deuono accomodare i bocci. oli à Luna mā cante, di modo che venghino à nascere i ver micelli al principio della crescente .

H Ponte Sant'Angelo.

I L'Inferno Torrion di Castello.

K Maschio del Castel Sant'Angelo.

M Torre Borgia.

L Torre Capitana.

P Teuere i iume.

Opposite: Women in the silk trade encouraged technological invention and benefited from increased commerce. Until the 16th century, raw silk was harvested from cocoons once per year. Meir Magino, a Venetian Jewish inventor, developed a process for extracting silk thread from cocoons twice per year. Pope Sixtus V invited Meir Magino to the Papal States in 1587 to introduce his marvelous techniques. The following year Magino published an elegantly printed, illustrated book in Italian with a Hebrew poem on his newly patented invention for silk-making. This illustration is from that book. [Magino also secured a patent for a polishing oil for mirrors and cut glass, and a grant of exclusive right to produce wine bottles, still used today in Roman wineshops.] Magino's daughters worked in the family silk business.

Chaucer relates that his Wife of Bath was so talented a clothmaker that she surpassed those of the clothmaking capitals of Ypres and Gaunt.

While clothmaking and embroidery were significant industries they were also noble pastimes, numerous important women practicing not for pay but recreation. Some embroidered for civic duty. The exquisite Bayeux Tapestry celebrating the events of 1066 generally is attributed to Queen Matilda. Numerous noblewomen and significant churchwomen were avocationally needle workers, adding to the production of their professional sisters such strong and delicate artistic creation so as to make Flanders and England capitals of the medieval needle-working world, and the phrase *opus Anglicanum* or "English work" the epithet for perfection in handiwork.

No matter how exquisitely woven or worked, much medieval cloth such as our cape and hood was further embellished. Women embellishers had high repute as decorators of cloth with gold and silver threads, glass and jet beads, copper sequins, pearls, semiprecious stones, and jewels. The acquisition of raw materials used by the embellishers also called for the vocations and talents of medieval craftswomen.

Copper mining and silver mining, significant medieval industries, employed women for many activities. Copper ore smelting and refining was ungendered work, women present both in the documents and portraits of foundries. Even more surprising is women's presence in and around the mines. Medieval women in certain countries apparently were miners as well as silver ore sorters and ore appraisers.

In paintings and documents of the Hungarian mining community of Kutna Hora women worked close to the mine pit head, although not in the tunnels below. Women ore washers and sorters stirred vats near the mine entrance. The miners working below in short leprechaunish hooded garments did not include women, but a document associated with a neighboring mine records payments to women for mining services underground.

Apparently medieval women miners practiced the same petty larcenies as their male colleagues. Required to strip nude before leaving the mine compound, miners could not easily conceal on their bodies any precious ore. However, documents record losses higher for women miners than men. Apparently a woman's anatomy permitted more places to hide precious contraband.

FOOD TRADESWOMEN

Imagine a beautiful, succulent 15th-century feast including among the poultry courses *swete feasaunt,* a delectable honey-glazed, stuffed pheasant served with piquant green sauce. Among the wines accompanying the beautiful bird is spiced claret, and among the fragrant breads is crisp rosepetal bread. That dinner could not be cooked without ingredients from women field workers, market sellers, and importers. An imaginary market tour to provide ingredients for these recipes demonstrates the prevalence of women working in all strata of the food trades.

In addition to bread and wine, our feast's ingredients list would require cheese, cherries, lentils, oats, salt, basil, and honey for the stuffing of the pheasant; for the sauce, white wine, spinach, and vinegar.

Shopping in the medieval market for fabulous feast fixings would have been logical, festive, and fragrant. London's markets were typical of many medieval towns wherein purveyors of one type of produce had their stalls and shops in a special area. In large towns like London, the vending area was an entire neighborhood. For silverware, we would look to the jewelry district; for bread, to Eastchepe Bread Street; for wine, to the Vintry; for our bird, we would go to the Poultry. Women not only sold the feast ingredients: earlier, women had produced them and carted them to the market.

Sold in Bread Street, the crisp-crusted delicately-hued rosepetal bread had its ultimate origins in the wheat and barley fields in which women labored hard and well. Some medieval women farmers simply worked their own family fields. Other women were hired laborers, paid wages similar to men farm hands. Yet others rented their lands from an overlord, or had obligations to harvest for an overlord, owing services to the landowner. A widowed or unmarried woman who was a "free tenant" or villein or cotter gave several days' free labor per week, certain services at harvest time, or hours of labor in planting, reaping, binding, threshing, winnowing, or thatching.

Working in fields with sickle and scythe, women grain gatherers sheathed and baled, preparing grain to carry to market or to transfer to women transporters. Selling to a baker or to a regrator, the grainwomen first might have the cereal milled into flour by a miller. Women millers were called millsters.

Women bakers, famous for excellent breads, were occasionally known to commit ingenious violations of the town laws regulating bread weight, quality, and cost. A pound loaf of rye or wheat, for instance, legally sold only for a certain price, and women bakers, as frequently as male colleagues, underweighed and overpriced merchandise. Their violations of the rules were prosecuted in the bread court, the *assize of bread*.

Brought to court by irate customers or town market officials, women were prosecuted for misrepresenting ingredients, for inserting small stones to make underweight breads weigh more, for wrapping good dough around a core of old stale dough, for adulterating good flour with bad, and for other bread frauds. These minor consumer fraud convictions led baxters to fines and punishments at the pillory. The market stocks especially for women malefactors were called the *thewe*.

More outrageous bread crimes were punished by drawing the lawbreaker through the streets on a sled, the illegal loaf tied around the neck. An amusing larceny among women public bakers to whose large ovens men and women brought their own dough for baking was dough-stealing by use of an ingeniously engineered table. (See page 119.)

Women bakers and bread regrators sold loaves round, oval, square, rectangular, octangular, flat, conical, braided, and pretzel-shaped. Rosepetal breads were beautifully colored light red; others were saffron-yellow and parsley-green. Some breads were fragrant with spices and herbs, others luscious with raisins, dates, citrons, glazed fruits, and candied vegetables.

Die sechßvndachtzigist figur

Opposite: A noble feaster dines alone at the high table while women courtiers eat at the long parallel refectory tables called sideboards, seated on benches according to social rank. Musicians play fanfares to announce the succession of courses, aid digestion, and augment culinary pleasure. A food servitor wearing a short tunic, tights, and extravagantly pointed shoes called poulaines *carries a stacked trio of covered dishes. Another servitor, the carver or the bread server, the* pantler, *wields a knife in his left hand and, with his right, offers a square bread slice on a spatula. The bread was the edible* trencher *or platter, usually colored delicate red with rosepetals, or green with parsley and rosemary, or gold with saffron. Foods were presented, placed upon, and eaten from the trencher which absorbed gravies and sauces. Leftovers were toasted and recycled as breakfast sops in wine or served to the dogs or to the poor begging culinary alms (*trencher fees*) at the castle gate. Elaborate finger choreography rather than forks conveyed food to the feasters' mouths. The first finger in opposition to the thumb were the meat fingers, the middle finger and thumb for fish, and the ring finger and thumb served fowl. Little fingers were spice fingers, dipped into salt, sugar, powdered mustard, or crushed herbs, and with sensual flourish, lifted to the lips. A credenza with two latched doors, called an* aumbry, *on the rear wall displays serving vessels. Some* aumbries *were lead-lined refrigerators or ice chests, commonly used in 15th-century dining halls for wines, ciders, or chilled desserts.*

Oat breads for people and for animals were bought from the ostler. A woman oat seller purveying her grains provided another requirement for the stuffing of *swete feasaunt.*

From Bread Street to the Vintry, women workers produced raw materials and sold finished products in wines and ales. In vineyards women planted grapes, cultivating them through harvest, selecting grapes for eating, cooking, preserving, or winemaking, and then fermenting the fruit, pressing the grapes into wine. Constantly checking for excellence or spoilage, women winemakers sold to taverners or to wine merchants, many of them women.

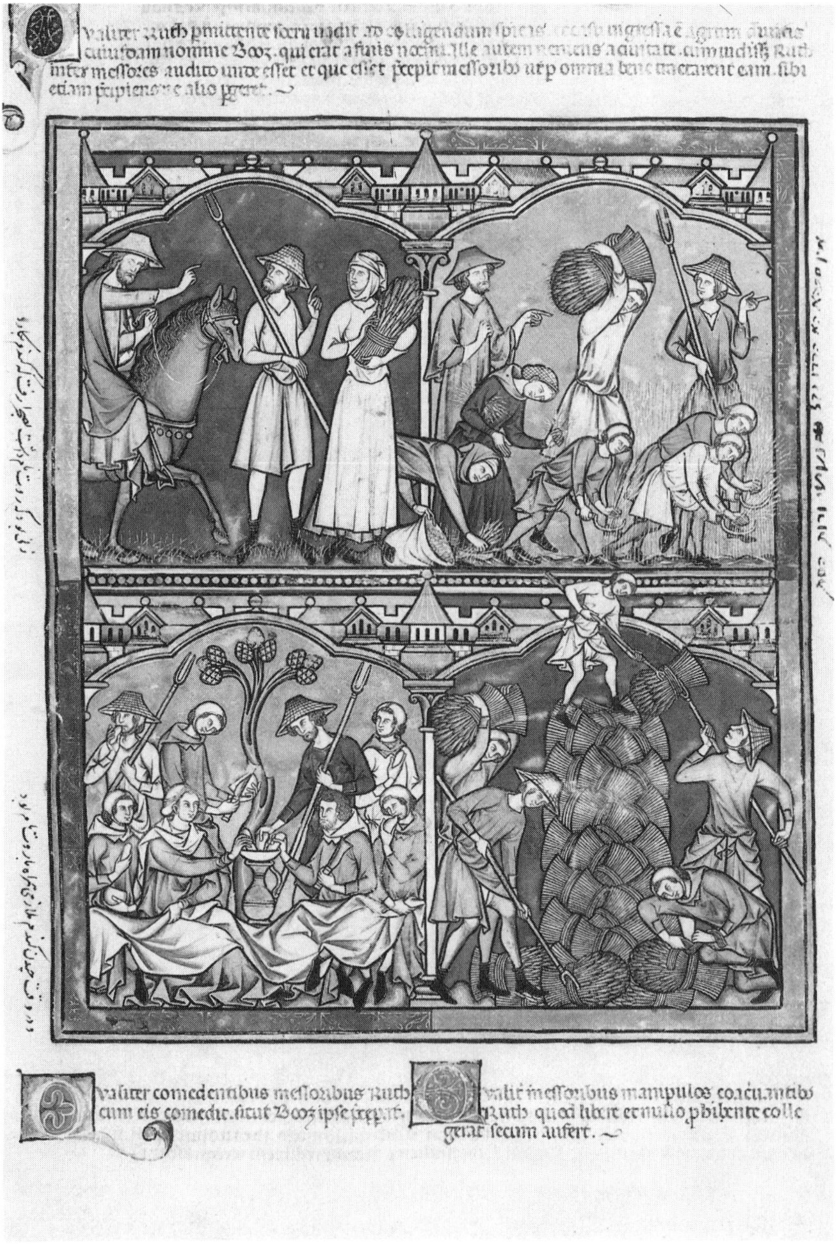

Opposite: Barley reapers cut grain with sickles before binding the grain in sheaves. Bound by cording or by barley stalks, the grain is stacked high in a tower of alternating sheaves. In the upper register the woman holding a bound sheaf is the Old Testament's Ruth, who appears again, at right, gleaning after the reapers cut the grain, and below, eating. The rural banquet cloth is spread across four pairs of knees while Ruth and Boaz dip their bread into vinegar set in a bowl atop a golden pitcher; two sun-hatted field workers with two-pronged mowing forks join the meal.

Imported red wine was had from France or Spain or Sicily and laid in separate wine cellars from the domestic white wines. Stringent rules controlled price and quality. Fourteenth-century London's wine shops stocked at least 56 French wines, and 30 varieties of Italian, Spanish, and Canarian. A red Tuscan wine called Vernaccia sold for no more than 2 shillings a gallon in 1350. Sixteen pence purchased a sweet Greek *Wine of Crete; Malveisin,* probably a malmsey, from Crete or Morea, and *Wine of the River.* Likewise at that price were the aromatic spiced wines such as *Piemente* and *Clare,* piment and claret.

The Vintry also was the source for vinegar, piquant or sour wine (*vin aigre*).

Women made malt beer and ale. The *assize of ale* preserves in its court documents large numbers of cases brought against women beer and ale makers and sellers. Scoundrel alewives were so common that they are a stock figure in carved church choir seats, the *misericords.* A misericord is the underside of a church pew fit for leaning on when a tired, long-standing choir singer merited "pity." Their carvings often portray an ale seller, naked and upside-down, carrying her fraudulent measuring cup as demons toss her into the mouth of Hell.

For the ricotta cheese for *swete feasaunt* a dairywoman, or as Chaucer calls her, a "daye," would sell produce probably from her own farm, or if a woman regrator, from other farmers' animals. Cow, sheep, and goat milk, creams, cheeses, plain butter, or spiced butters were by law allowed to be sold only at particular hours and at specific locations in order to assure freshness and avoid spoilage. Ricotta had to be purchased before the market clock struck 3 P.M.

Women fruit harvesters supplied the cherries for *swete feasaunt,* and the spinach for its sauce. Working several crafts simultaneously, a spinach harvester or orange picker might also be a spinster carrying her distaff. Oranges from Seville graced the fruit stands. Vendors advertised their wares with street cries such as: "Oranges, sweet oranges! Buy my oranges!"

Prodigious numbers of fresh fruits and vegetables, domestic and imported, were available in medieval markets, fresh in season and dried or candied. Women and men fruit sellers purveyed varieties of apple, pear, strawberry, orange, quince, melon, grape, whortleberry, mulberry, plum, peach, service, pomegranate, and the ubiquitous carob, St. John's bread. These, fresh from tree or vine, were sold next to dried date, fig, raisin, currant, and prune.

To reach the displays of spinach, in its many varieties, it was necessary to pass arrays of lettuce, cabbage, green beans, peas dried and fresh, carrot, celery, cucumber, parsnip, radish, garlic, leek, artichoke, chicory, endive, beets, olives, onions, lentils, and turnips.

Next: the condiments. Women spicers offered honey, domestic and imported from as far away as Russia, and numerous sugars and salts of various shapes, textures, and colors. Gardens of fragrant leaves, seeds, berries, and barks perfumed the market. Basil, borage, dittany, mallow, oregano, fennel, cardamom, sorrel, pennyroyal, galingale, clove, hyssop, mandragora, licorice, purslane, mustard seed (in prodigal varieties), nutmeg, peppercorn, pine seed, cubeb, sandalwood, cinnamon, clove—available in forms whole, powdered, liquid, stick, chunk, cake, grain, coarse-ground, light-ground, and crystalline—created a spicery wildly aromatic.

The crucial ingredient for *swete feasaunt* is the bird itself. The Poultry was the next market after the meat market (called the *shambles,* meaning

One woman farmer squats to milk her cow. So long as she adheres to strict market laws governing the sale of perishable dairy products, she can sell milk, cream, butter, and cheese at market. Another farmer tends her cow in a barn. In the adjoining barn a woman farmer churns butter made from either cow milk or sheep milk. The man at right helps sheep out of a sheepcote while a herder wearing shorts carries a young lamb.

slaughterhouse). Women brought freshly killed animals for display and sale. In the Shambles, women butchers, like men butchers, cut and trimmed, cured and smoked, sold and wrapped the meat of sheep, pig, cow, ox, deer, bear, beaver, wolf, and rabbit, and sometimes whale and porpoise. Before reaching the market, those meats were bodies of animals hunted by both men and women, killing for profit as well as for pleasure. Boar and bear were hunted by women and men as private exercises of the rich. But hunters' quarry reached the kitchen and huntresses' kills also were for market. Smaller game such as rabbit, men and women caught with nets and ferrets.

The Poultry's many types of fowl matched the Shambles' variety of meats. Beyond the expected hen, rooster, goose, gander, and the young pullets of each, larger and smaller fowl were raised, caught, netted, shot by arrow, or hunted by hawks. Birds brought to market included bittern, bustard, crane, curlew, and dove. Likewise, eagle, egret, gull, heron, lark, mallard, partridge, peacock, pigeon, plover, and quail. As popular for feast menus were sparrow, shoveler, snipe, sarcelle, stork, swan, teal, whimbrel, and woodcock. The pheasant in the Poultry might have been a domestic fowl raised by a woman farmer or a wild one caught by a man or woman falconer.

Gorgeous market colors and odors, and long walks among food stalls, aisles, and streets might make shoppers hungry for a quick meal, ready to go. One of the nearby inns or prepared food shops would be open at most hours of the day and night. A 12th-century food shop near London Bridge sold exotic, foreign delicacies fully prepared for eating in or taking out, and was open even on Sundays.

The *swete feasaunt* shopping list's final item was charcoal for the stove and ovens which could be bought from a charcoal seller, the last food market tradeswoman to visit.

Since horsepower was the major engine of conveyance on land, a trip to the blacksmith was necessary if the horse needed to be reshod. Just as medieval marketwomen had transported their produce by horseback paniers or by horse and wagon, so the shopper entrusting the feast preparations to a horse-drawn cart must examine the horses' shoes. A woman smith called a *farris* worked alone at her trade, or she might work in partnership with her husband, or as his assistant. Women forged iron and worked in many metal crafts, from the mining of silver to the pulling and working of delicate filigree.

onchata e lacte coagulato e fredo
e humido el migliore sie de aiali gioueni
mangiato giona ala extinatioe del stomacho
e cura la sete Noce che fa fastidio e graua
lo stomacho aremouere el nocumeto mangiata
con senapre e sale

pinachi sono fredi in primo grado
li migliori sono per la pioua man
guar giouano ala tosse e al pecto noceno
che impedisero la digestione fremouere
el nocimeto parati col sale

A 15th-century spinach seller, bound by town law to sell fresh produce at particular times in specific market places, served citizens' hygiene as well as cuisine. Foods and drinks were thought to have medicinal purposes. The unlearned who knew inherited food folklore and the learned who knew empirical scientific data selected fruits and vegetables, as well as fish, poultry, and meats, not simply to please taste but to prevent, treat, or cure disease. In medical texts, herbals, and health manuals, spinach was thought especially effective against coughs and chest congestion. It also was recommended as nourishing for young people and those with "warm" temperaments. Ideally, shoppers selected foods at their "optimum" time for creating dishes and menus for medical effect. This woman produce seller depicted in a Tacuinum Sanitatis (Table of health) carries in a basket balanced on her head the spinach leaves picked at optimum time, when wet with rainwater, and "cold and humid in the first degree." Spinach's possible "danger" in disturbing the digestion could be neutralized by sautéing it with salt water, or with vinegar and aromatic herbs.

MATRONYMICS

Children of market bakers, cooks, brewers, poulterers, and craftswomen appear by name in medieval documents identified by the profession of their mothers: Jonathan, son of Elizabeth le Baxter; Matilde, daughter of Joan Brewster; Louis, son of Eva Webster. These names persist today. Yet the heritage of women's work and women's achievements often is denied. Three interrelated issues require consideration. Why were children identified by their mothers' work; related to that, why did their names persist in matronymics? Why were women in 12th- through 15th-century Europe celebrated for their work, and, related to that, why in later centuries were their medieval achievements relegated to legend or condemned as inconsequential? Why in the early Middle Ages, say the 10th through 12th centuries, were women cherished, lauded, and "valued" equal to men, and related to that, why in some locales were women more "valuable" than men?

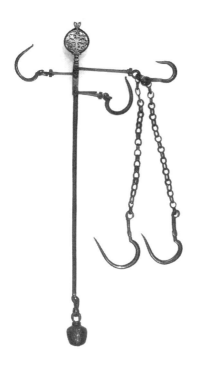

Steelyard scales weighed heavy produce, such as animal carcasses, sides of meat, or bales of wool. Produce was hung on a hook at the end of strong chains, and a weight slid along a calibrated post. Scales, measures, and weights throughout European market towns and cities were regulated by local or national authority, inspected, and stamped for authentic measure. To assure the integrity of commerce and to protect consumers against false weights and measures, regulations controlled scale makers and users. Violators were prosecuted in market courts and if convicted, forfeited goods or lost their licenses to sell commodities within particular jurisdictions. The Steelyard was the German quarter in medieval London where merchants from Cologne had rights and freedoms from tax granted by King Henry II in the 12th century, and later ratified by his successors. Warehouses, weighing houses, banks, a court, a church, and dwellings within the walls of the original Steelyard expanded when merchants from Lübeck and Hamburg added their mercantile power to London. After Queen Elizabeth expelled the Hanseatic League at the end of the 16th century, Steelyard commercial power vanished from England, but their scales' strength and design became emblems of strict, fair measure

Why matronymics evolved may be the simplest of the three questions to speculate upon. Families identified themselves by their mother's work because of the woman's significant economic function. Her fame in the market might have been easier to identify than her husband's because she did what she did better than he did what he did. Or she worked at a profession or craft socially honored while he did not. *Honos alit artes omnesque incenditur ad studia gloria,* Cicero said in his *Tusculan Disputations* (I,ii,4): public honor stimulates the arts and people are fired to fame by approval. Those arts are neglected that are less appreciated. If the mother was a working widow, her craft fed and therefore distinguished her family.

Another reason modern family names preserve both matronymics and patronymics may be that it is inevitable that people's work identifies them, both women and men. Modern prejudice in expecting only paternal wealth from paternal professions makes the "medieval natural" appear now as unnatural. Perhaps we should apply Ockham's Razor, that sharp, sure method the great philosopher William of Ockham created for deciding among unknowns until proof can be got. Of all the possibilities the simplest is the best. Women worked. Women worked well. Women gained fame for their work. Men worked. Men worked well. Men gained fame for their work. Some children of women and men were named by their mother's profession. Some children of men and women were named by their father's profession.

In illicit clerical families, priests who had vowed celibacy nevertheless fathered children. For families of married priests, common before the 10th century, secrecy about paternity often was expedient. Therefore identifying the children by their mother's work was reasonable, especially since her work usually assured the family's financial survival. Priests recorded their praise of their women's work in aghast reaction to a 10th-century decree requiring them to abandon their wives. Unless "maintained by the hands of their women, they would succumb to hunger and nakedness." Both the warrior and the priest needed freedom from "domestic solicitude" to pursue affairs of state or soul. Their professional requirements elevated woman's social prominence and encouraged the transmission of women's professional names.

LAW, DEMOGRAPHY, AND PERSONAL VALUE

Addressing questions of women's worth between the 10th and 15th centuries in Europe requires excursions into law, demography, and pale-

*T*wo trussed birds roast on a mechanized spit, two footed cauldrons are heated above the fire's coals, and a large, heavy cauldron is suspended on a racking crook, a chain with a hook above an open fire, while one cook tastes from a ladle in his right hand and with his left hand stirs with a slotted spoon. Above the woman's head are two round-headed, long-handled peles, resembling modern pizza paddles, for inserting and removing loaves and pastries in deep ovens.

opathology. Differences between earlier and later medieval "valuation" of women can best be understood by reviewing pre-12th-century laws that protected women's value and actually celebrated a woman's worth with a monetary price on her life—which was hard and short.

Laws of an early Germanic tribe, the Salian Franks, required that if a person were killed, the killer had to pay to the bereaved family a special fine called *weregild* (man-money or "people-gold"). The *weregild* for the murder of a man was 200 solidi, whatever his age. If the murder victim was a girl who was not old enough to conceive children, the *weregild* was still 200 solidi. But after the woman began to work and to bear children, her *weregild* tripled to 600 solidi, and there remained until old age. The penalty for killing a pregnant woman was 700 solidi. A very old woman's *weregild* reverted to the normal male charge of 200 solidi. During her working, child-bearing years a woman was "worth" more than a man of the same age and social rank. During her working and child-bearing years every ordinary woman enjoyed the same protection, the same monetary value, accorded the king's companions and Christian bishops.

Another Germanic tribe, the Alamans, so cherished women for their work and their childbearing that laws specially protected women, from womb to tomb. If a man attacked a pregnant woman, causing her to abort a fetus, the fine for that reprehensible act would be 12 solidi if the child were male, 24 solidi if female. Loss of a baby girl was twice as grave as loss of a baby boy. Fines for any injury to women were double those for men. Fines doubled even for robbing the grave of a woman. Perhaps women were buried with jewelry their husbands gave them as gifts at marriage.

Such a marriage gift was a dowry brought by a husband to a wife. Called the *morgengabe,* the gift of the new day, the gift of the morning, it was the valuables the new husband gave to his wife on the morning after their first night in bed.

Such rules and customs suggest the workings of the marketplace. Women were valued highly because they were scarce. While today women outnumber men, it was not always so. Analyses of medieval ratios of women to men demonstrate that in the early Middle Ages there were too few women to go around for all the ready and eager men.

Not only were there fewer women than men in Europe right through the 15th century but women seem to have had a shorter life expectancy than men. While the paleopathology record is unclear, excavations of medieval women's graves suggest that on average women died earlier than similarly situated men. Even in the late classical period women's care of the "house, hearth, and fields," as Tacitus phrased it, left them little time for life. The life expectancy for the early medieval woman was dismally short. Apparently Aristotle's idea that men live longer than women held true until somewhere around the 11th century.

Nevertheless, soon after the 12th century, women began to outnumber men, a demographic circumstance persisting to this day. Why? Perhaps because towns and codes of chivalry made existence less perilous. Perhaps effective town and state government could give greater protection and personal security against rape and abduction. Women free of certain forms of violence lived longer.

Records show that in 15th-century Nuremberg, there were 1,207 women for every 1,000 men; in Basle, 1,246 women for every 1,000 men. Women who might have been happy to be wives had no available men to marry. Women's choices then were a convent or a craft.

When women were more plentiful, they became less precious, and less valuable. When women became the majority, they became a threat.

SILK AND WOOL CRAFTSWOMEN

Silkwomen in London petitioned the crown in 1368 against competition from alien men, particularly the Lombards. The long preamble to their request to restrict imports of silk begins: "The silkwomen and threwstresses of the craft and occupation of silkwork within the city of London, which has been the craft of women within the same city so long a time that no one says to the contrary, that before now, many a worshipful woman within the city has lived full honorably and therewith many good households kept and many gentlewomen and others in great numbers, probably more than 1,000, have been learning as apprentices under them the same crafts and occupation, full virtuously under the pleasance of God . . ." insisted that the Italian silk be kept out of London. Their petition was successful.

Under the jurisdiction of London's silkwomen, 14th-century apprentices worked for between seven and 15 years. If the silk mistress was married, indentures for the apprentice were drawn up either in her name alone or in her name and her husband's name, but always specifying that it was her trade and not his which was to be taught. The young girl or boy apprentice promised to diligently study the craft, to never divulge craft secrets, and to behave well, avoiding stealing, inappropriate frivolity, running away, sexual relations, and marrying. Families of apprentices often were coerced into lending the mistress money as trading capital. Since noblemen apprenticed daughters to the lucrative silk trade, the silkwomen masters sometimes arranged spectacular financial transactions.

In Italy many silkwomen belonged to politically important families, amassing international mercantile fortunes. In the 15th century, one prominent man petitioning to allow his own sister into this lucrative profession was the pope.

Not only silk but wool craftswomen, such as the merchant Rose of Burford, gained renown. Born into a wealthy English family, Rose of Burford married a rich merchant, soon sheriff of London. He had made a huge loan in 1368 to King Edward III for fighting his Scots wars. Rose's husband died before the King repaid his debt. As executor of her husband's will, Rose tried to extract the money from the reluctant king, five times petitioning for the money in court.

Exasperated, she suggested that the king allow her freedom from paying customs duty on wool that she was ready to ship out from the port of London. Appearing in court with the documents correctly demonstrating the king's debt, she was excused that total sum from the duties she otherwise would have paid. Her savings in customs payments of the amount equal to the fortune her husband had lent the king suggests the magnitude of her wool empire.

JEWISH CRAFTSWOMEN

Letters of Jewish traders and merchants describing women at work in importing and exporting are preserved in the Cairo Geniza. That astonishing collection of letters, contracts, accounts, court proceedings, business ledgers, family letters, and personal jottings dating from the 10th through the 13th centuries is preserved in the lumber room adjacent to the main synagogue of Cairo. Part of a Jewish garbage heap preserved because papers bearing the name of God could be disposed of only by burial and not burning, this treasure trove of detritus from medieval Jewish culture in the Mediterranean was brought in part to Cambridge University by the scholar Solomon Schecter in the 19th century.

A letter from 1170 in the Geniza was written to the famous physician-philosopher Moses Maimonides by David, his younger brother. David was an import-export trader. He had just endured the perils of crossing the desert between the Nile and the Red Sea to reach the Sudanese port of Aydhab, reputed for its important markets.

As translated by Solomon Goitein: "To my beloved brother Moses Maimon your brother David writes with troubled mind. After Passover I booked for Aydhab in a caravan. But I was forced to travel the desert alone with only one companion in this disastrous undertaking. The hardships were unfathomable but the two of us survived, safely with our entire baggage. When I arrived at the town I found nothing to buy except indigo. Having survived with God's blessing that perilous crossing of the sands I decided I would have little to risk by crossing the sea to India. My companions in the Malabar Sea will be Salim, the son of the woman broker, and his brother's son, Makarim, and the brother of Lady Gazelle (the broker). Do not worry, He who saved me from the desert will save me on the sea. Written on the 22nd of Iyyar while the express caravan is ready to leave."

The letter was the last David wrote before he drowned in the Indian Ocean. But apart from the poignancy of its context, it provides glimpses into the Jewish mercantile world of the time. It is testimony to the importance of women commodity brokers, and to the fact that their sons were identified by their mothers' professions. Women were among the significant medieval Jewish traders whose influence extended beyond their local towns and merchandise fairs to as far away as Africa and India.

Not far from Cambridge the delightful medieval town of Bury St. Edmunds has still standing a solid 12th-century stone house called Moyse's Hall. By tradition it is a Jew's house. Apparently it was owned by a Jewish mercantile woman between the years 1154 and 1189. Jews in Bury St. Edmunds thrived, partly because of the reasonably benevolent reign of King Henry II and Queen Eleanor.

In this small provincial town Jews worked as successful bankers. Since the medieval church condemned money lending for interest as the sin of usury, many prominent bankers were Jews. Moreover, Jews could grant credit to each other and enforce contracts in the rabbinic courts. Therefore major capitalists such as Aaron of Lincoln could back the smaller moneylenders by bond, allowing them to sell at a discount. Amassing huge fortunes which were heavily taxed by King Henry and

Eleanor, these Jewish moneylenders offered excellent sources of revenue both to the borrower and to the King's coffers.

Thriving Jewish moneylenders included women. Their names appear frequently in the calendar of *Plea Rolls of the Exchequer of the Jews,* as money brokers, as widows of moneylenders carrying on their husband's profession, and as landlords who also were money brokers renting out their stout stone houses.

Most houses owned by Jews in Bury St. Edmunds and in Norwich seem to have been leased under the woman's name as landlord. Perhaps this was to enable widows to avoid the high death tax on an estate amounting to one-third of the total inheritance otherwise due to the king. Moyse's Hall apparently was such a merchant Jew's house owned by a woman moneylender of Bury.

WEALTHY WIDOWED CRAFTSWOMEN

Wealthy widowed Jewish or Christian tradeswomen, who created wealth by their own hands or by inheritance from their husbands, often parlayed their fortunes into nobility. Such widows had to fend off proposals from merchantmen, gentlemen, and noble suitors eager for their fortunes. Christine de Pizan in her *Book of the Three Virtues* has advice for rich townswomen chased by eager admirers. Widows wishing to preserve their good names must behave appropriately, avoiding clothing too tight, too low-cut, too flashy, too costly, or too suggestive. Such clothes attract men. By bearing, countenance, and clothing, the medieval merchantwoman might succeed in avoiding those who are attracted to her for her wealth but in whom she has little interest.

However, if an aggressively offensive man persists, then Christine rehearses precisely what a widow should say: "Sir, if you have any respect for me, I ask you politely to withdraw. I swear to you that I have no interest in a love affair with you. Nor will I ever. You are wasting your time and trouble if you persist. Please stop looking at me that way and stop talking to me. I will try as best I can never to go where you are. I tell you this once for all. Goodbye." (*Book of the Three Virtues* III, 22)

Court records describe wealthy businesswomen who are widowed playing off one suitor against another. For instance, a draper, a dry goods and fabric merchant, had made a marriage contract with a widow. For three years he spent much time and money on her business, as he said in a court testimony, intending that his expenses would redound to his own "benefit and profit in time to come."

In the same spirit he gave her numerous gifts of which he kept a very careful account: a pair of great beads gilded with gold worth 2 pounds 2 shillings; a huge ring of fine gold with a large pointed diamond, 10 pounds; a small chain of gold; a gold signet ring with her arms engraved in stone with a ruby and emerald.

Moreover, he spent a great deal of money entertaining her friends and buying them New Year's presents. She even sent him to Spain to buy large quantities of merchandise for her.

While he was away, she dallied with one of his rivals. On his return from Spain she refused to marry him. She declined even to see him. Try as he might, she would not give him her hand.

So he tried to gain the upper hand in finances when the rich widow died, unexpectedly and unmarried. The draper rushed to court and successfully claimed her huge fortune.

Whether widows of culinary or clothier craftsmen, married craftswomen, *femmes soles,* or girl apprentices from upper or lower classes training for the lucrative food and cloth trades, skillful dedicated women professional workers mightily affected the economies of their countries, their families, and their private lives. These craftswomen were known not by their work alone but by their work primarily.

5

WOMEN IN
ILLICIT TRADES

fictional 15th-century English tavern in Surrey is owned by the extraordinary brew mistress Eleanor Rumming. Her inn attracts customers from afar for its potent, delectable beer and ale. At all hours on all days craftswomen come for the super brew, the tunning of Eleanor Rumming. She serves the prostitute, thief, murderer, scold, fraud, farm wife, weaver, astrologer, woman doctor, and at least one witch. Here medieval England's women of the illicit trades are swilling, guzzling, bibbling, miming, stinking, swearing, lying, conniving, reeling, stealing, pealing laughter, and peeling their clothes off. To this woman's brew house come women in their salad days, green in judgment. Old women join Eleanor herself—over-ripe, rank toward rotting, yet jubilant.

John Skelton, laureate, poet, translator, tutor, ordained to holy orders, created Eleanor's rabble. Perhaps he wrote "The Tunning of Eleanor Rumming" for his pupil, that intelligent, lascivious boy, later King Henry VIII. Eleanor's tavern is a frame tale for the laws, court cases, scurrilous stories, and portraits of medieval women in the illicit trades. Of the canny, feisty, exultant old hostess, Eleanor Rumming, Skelton wrote:

Her loathly lere
Is nothing clear,
But ugly of cheer,
Droopy and drowsy,
Scurvy and lousy,
Her face all bowsy,
Comely crinkled,
Wondrously wrinkled,
Like a roast pig's ear
Bristled with hair
She is ugly fair.

But to make up my tale,
She brews a nappy ale,
And makes thereof pot-sale
To travellers, to tinkers,
To sweaters, to swinkers,
And all good ale-drinkers,
That will nothing spare
But drink till they stare
And bring themselves bare.

Sluts of lewd sort
To Eleanor resort.

Eleanor, I thee pray
Of thine ale let us essay
And have here a pilch of gray:
I wear skins of coney,
That causeth I look so donny!"

Now in comes another rabble:
First one with a ladle,
Another with a cradle,
And with a side-saddle;
And there began a fabble,
A clattering and babble
Of foolish Philly
That had a foal with Willy.
She could not lie stilly.

PROSTITUTES

The distinction between professional practitioner and good amateur often is simply place of business and uniform. Medieval prostitutes usually practiced in certain restricted districts. The women were routinely examined by local health authorities for venereal disease. They were required to wear special identifying garb. In 14th-century London, the red-light district was called the Stewes, on the far side of the Thames in Bankside, Southwerk. A second whorehouse area was called Cokkeslane in Smithfield. Cokkeslane might refer to poultry or to genitalia.

A Norman-French law dated 1393 delineates the reasons for establishing the sex neighborhood, the isolation of the sex trade to assigned areas, and the penalties for craftswomen who violate the rules. "Whereas many diverse frays, broils, and dissentions have arisen in time past and many men have been slain and murdered, by reason of the frequent resort to and consorting with common harlots at taverns, brew houses of hucksters, and other places of ill fame within the city. And more especially through Flemish women who profess to such shameful, dolorous life. We forbid that any such women should move about or lodge in the city or its suburbs, by night or by day. But they are to keep themselves to the assigned places, the Stewes and Cokkeslane. On pain of losing and forfeiting the upper garment that she shall be wearing, together with her hood, every time found contrary to this proclamation."

Sumptuary law precisely prescribed and proscribed medieval whores' cloaks and hoods. They were permitted to wear only certain colors of outer garment made only of particular fabrics and furs. Proclamations of 1351 and 1382 complained against common lewd women from foreign places, dwelling in London, who assumed the fashions and attire of good, noble dames and damsels of the realm. This unreasonable disguise of their profession and inappropriate class-climbing by clothes thenceforth was forbidden.

"No lewd women," says this law, may be attired by day or night in any gowns trimmed in such furs as miniver, grey badger, *puree of stranlyng,* spring or fall or winter squirrel, brown rabbit lambskin or hare fur. Furthermore, whores may not wear garments lined with sendal, rich textured Samite silk, or any other noble lining, either in winter or in summer.

But every "common lewd woman" going about the city by day or night must wear with her cape a cloth hood, of the special fabric called *ray,* neither trimmed nor lined. All folk, native and stranger, then will know what rank she is.

Strict sumptuary laws allocated costumes to whores just as they distinguished other professions, social classes, and religions. For example, in certain areas Jews were required to wear the pointed hat called the "Judenhut," or to wear a special circular identification badge, the rouelle, on their outer garments, or to wear purple shoes. Medical men and women were to dress in long red capes and tunics, the arms lined with fur or satin.

Likewise, Italian prostitutes of Bologna were required to sport the unlined ray-hood; adornments and slashes were permitted on their sleeves but not on their gowns. Rome's richer courtesan costumes were more flamboyant, the permissible decorations and jewels more generous than in Venice. There, as in London, special indoor clothing prescriptions were complemented by outdoor clothing regulations. Moreover, the true Venetian brothel prostitute was distinguishable by garb from the less professional street-walker. Whores from the island of Rhodes wore their heritage in their dress. Eastern women were thought the more fetchingly alluring in their own costumes. The customer knew by these sex practitioners' clothes the caliber of the service he was purchasing.

The medieval red-light district was as orderly and exuberant as reasonably could be expected. Whorehouses intermingled among eating and drinking establishments often were disguised as bath houses, uniting stimulating food with erotic festivity. Prostitutes sponge-bathed their customers with fragrant water while feeding them aphrodisiac foods such as clams, pears, or chestnuts cooked in cream. In communal baths the women and men drank naked, except for their hats and jewels. Fine spiced wines excited libidinous interest.

In some pleasure houses men and women dallied nude in heated perfumed waters, each couple in its own velvet-covered bathing vessel, the banquet table set before them. A special heating apparatus kept the water caressingly warm. With sensuous music and titillating delicacies, the cavorters floated their desires from the bath to the bed.

Many medieval baths were respectable entertainment palaces in which friendly or married couples delighted in swimming and eating together. Others were places of such licentiousness and erotic perversity that many cities banned baths altogether. Complainants generally were the civil authorities or the church. The sexual ingenuities of bath patrons, plus their occasional associated crimes of assault, battery, thievery, and larceny, distressed the city peacekeepers and elected authorities.

In 1417, for example, London's city council insisted upon the abolition of the Stewes district in the City. Councilmen complained of the "grievances, abominations, damages, disturbances, murders, homicides, larcenies, and other common nuisances befallen London because of the common resort, harboring, and sojourning in the Stewes of lewd men and women of bad and evil life." Lamentably, diverse men and women there had been "slain, spoiled, and robbed."

Even worse, the wives, sons, apprentices, and servants of reputable men of the City had been enticed into the houses by the Stewe-owners and profiteers. There they indulged in "illicit works of their lewd flesh" to the "great abomination and displeasure of God and to the great dishonor and damages of the City." For these reasons, the Stewes were to be removed forever.

Apparently one of London's aldermen, Robert Chichele, may have been less spurred by moral indignation than by imperatives of real-estate profit. As part of a deal with the City fathers to remove the whorehouses, he gave London considerable land, tenements, and appurtenances in Surrey amounting to the substantial yearly income of 40 marks. Twenty marks were to be paid annually to himself and his wife so long as they lived. Perhaps as the City of London expanded, the red-light district—originally distant from the major financial center—became desirable

Feasting on sexually stimulating wines and aphrodisiacs set on a banquet board straddling the gunwales of their independent bathing vessels, men and women eat while seated in warm, fragrant waters, naked except for their jewels and hats. Physicians advanced the proposition that thwarted sexuality was bad for mental health. A musician plays the lute. The sensual bathhouse repertoire included a shivaree, whose rhythms and melodies, customarily played at weddings as well, were thought stimulating to artful coupling.

development property for such politically astute entrepreneurs as Robert Chichele. His lavish gift to the City may have been a financial bribe for its condemning the whores' district, making the properties available for sale. He had first option.

Another 15th-century ordinance forbade landlords to harbor as tenants any persons of "evil and vicious life." This law explicitly asserted the financial complicity of some City officials in whore-mongering. Men or women indicted for bad and pernicious life lived in houses belonging not only to commoners but to aldermen. For profit, landlords permitted "illicit works of carnal appetites," there wasting honest wealth upon "heinous sins and the most abominable deeds imaginable." Thenceforth, no one was allowed to receive as tenant or allow to remain in tenantry any man or woman indicted, charged, or known to be of "evil and vicious life."

The Stewes, at least officially, were banned. But only for a time. They seem not to have been dreadfully disrupted. Just as prostitutes wore garments that defied the laws, so their houses flouted the law or were easily disguised as other than what they are. Evidence suggests that despite ordinances and bans, the Stewes and Cokkeslane thrived.

Just as sexual business establishments could be disguised, so also could private practitioners, the harlot masquerading as housekeeper. Many complaints were brought against Richard de Ker of Wacksfield, who kept a "loose woman" in his house. In court Richard insisted that though the harlot lived in, he had hired her to bring up his children, having no sexual relations with her whatsoever. Observant investigators found otherwise.

Hidden whore lore pervades medieval nursery rhymes. As with most nursery ditties, the simple surface hid a political or moral message. A nursery rhyme speaking of that fine piece of domestic furniture, the king's cushion, obliquely refers to that which the king lies down upon, namely, his paid mistress. Likewise, children skipping rope innocently sing: "Here I am/little jumping Joan/ When nobody is with me/ I'm all alone." They unwittingly sing the whore's invitation to seduction.

Procuresses and madams in medieval London did brisk business. Whore leaders came from all social classes, providing services for commoners, kings, and clerics. Sometimes they worked in their own house; otherwise they arranged rental services, or performed in the customer's home. The procuress kept the full fee for nightly service, allotting to the whore a salary either per month, per day, or more usually, per night. Madams trained their girls as apprentices, just as craftswomen trained the next generation of practitioners in the food and clothing trades.

One professional craft occasionally cloaked another. Elizabeth, wife of the prominent Londoner Henry Moring, appears in legal documents as a master embroiderer so respected she taught her techniques to others. In 1385 Elizabeth was brought to court because her serving woman Johanna confessed that Elizabeth took Johanna into her home, and numerous other women also, pretending to teach them the craft of embroidery, binding them to her service as apprentices. In truth, however, she did not follow that needle-craft but retained them "to live a lewd life, and to consort with friars, chaplains, and all other such men as desired to have their company, as well in their own house as elsewhere."

Elizabeth hired out her girls to those same friars, chaplains, and other men for such stipulated sum as they might agree upon, retaining the proceeds herself. One evening Elizabeth sent Johanna with a chaplain to his own quarters to spend the night. When Johanna returned the next morning, her mistress Elizabeth asked what she had brought for her labors that night, *pro labore suo*. Johanna had received no fee. Elizabeth was furious, ordering her back to the chaplain the following night to lay her hands on anything she could "for her trouble," and to return with the booty the next morning.

Johanna carried off the chaplain's valuable prayer book, which Elizabeth then sold for cash. Elizabeth received like "base gains" from Johanna and her other serving women. The court documents describe Elizabeth, living thus "abominably and damnably," as a whorehouse madam inciting other women to live in the same manner, herself a "common harlot and a procuress."

The popular prostitute often had scheduling difficulties. Unless resorting to orgies, the sex practitioner had to schedule eager clients efficiently so as not to interfere with their pleasures or her profits. Reminiscent of Geoffrey Chaucer's superb "Miller's Tale" of a bawdy young wife entertaining her college-student-lover while her old husband temporarily, safely snores in a tub, Masuccio in 1475 tells a variant form of that marvelous fabliau in which a beautiful, extravagantly sexual young woman dallies and deals with multiple lovers and customers, exercising three men during the same night. This fiction may exaggerate or reflect reality.

Sumptuous Viola's three favorite lovers are, first, her neighbor the blacksmith; second, a Genoese merchant; and third, a church friar, an expert, notorious adventurer. Promising all three to oblige them that same night, she arranges first with the Genoese merchant because he is the most ardent lover. She agrees to have dinner with him and to give him lodging. For this he makes her most extravagant promises. Viola schedules him for after dark, about 7 P.M.

Joyfully, he secretly sends two extra large capons, fresh bread, and excellent wines to the young woman's house for their precoital feast.

The friar eager for fulfillment, Viola arranges to meet at 11 P.M. She delays the blacksmith until dawn by stating, "Dear, you know how disliked I am in this neighborhood and how all the women with good reason are trying to get rid of me. Some of them spy on me even in the middle of the night. To prevent my being caught in their snares, wait until dawn. Signal me to let you in."

At early nightfall the Genoese merchant enters Viola's house. Though given a joyous reception and many kisses, his sluggish nature does not permit him to satisfy his fleshly appetites without certain inducements in the warmth of a bed. Mounting his steed, he begins to go through his paces. However, the young woman is terribly anxious, fearing to be anticipated by the second course before she has savored the first. Nine o'clock has already struck, and their dinner was not even begun.

They hear a knock at the door. The merchant, greatly alarmed, and more timorous than hot with love, takes refuge outside on the bedroom window ledge. Viola locks him out.

To the knocking importunate friar Viola says: "You have come too early and have not followed my direction." Nevertheless, the friar is so avid he does not even lock the door. He gives her plenary absolution on the spot. He is stimulated not by the authority vested in him by his superior, but by the strength granted by his own potent nature.

Viola, thinking this enough to satisfy him, sends him on his way. Instead he goes upstairs, warms himself in the bedroom, embraces Viola once again, beginning a new dance with a pleasanter melody. The Genoese merchant outside the window ledge sees everything. The friar, kindled by the pleasure of the beautiful girl, teaches Viola numbers of new dance steps. He also instructs the peeking Genoese merchant, until 4 o'clock. Then the blacksmith makes a commotion at Viola's door.

A practical joker, the friar sees a chance for fun. Imitating Viola's high-pitched voice he says, "I cannot open the door because it will make too much noise. There will be a scandal." The smith begs her to open up because he is burning with love for her.

Hearing this, the friar says in his high voice, "My beloved, give me a little kiss through this crack while I try to get this cursed door open quietly." The smith all agog makes ready for the kiss. The friar lets down his pants and sticks out his nether mouth.

Expecting to kiss Viola's sweet lips, the blacksmith immediately realizes by touch and smell what it really is. Immediately he vows revenge. Returning to his workshop, forging an iron rod, and heating it well, he has his apprentice keep it red hot. When the smith returns for a second kiss, the friar proffers him the same orifice. The blacksmith thrusts hard with the red hot iron.

So fierce is the blow, that the friar utters a yell, roaring like a wounded bull. Thereupon the Genoese merchant outside the window hears the clamor, sees the lights go on in the neighborhood, and jumps down from the high window ledge, breaking his leg.

The blacksmith and his apprentice carry the Genoese merchant to his lodgings. Next the blacksmith puts the friar with the roasted bottom on his shoulders and carries him to his monastery. Then he returns to his dear Viola at dawn, as per appointment, eats with her the succulent capons, and otherwise completely satisfies both their desires.

Clever Viola provided for all three lovers in one and the same night. She received absolution several times from the venerable priest. With him she taught the onlooking merchant and the smith the fashionable new dances.

The reform of prostitutes exercised the ingenuity of numerous churchmen who established organizations for saving and reforming degenerate women, such as the Order of Saint Mary Magdalene. Secular theorists also had regeneration schemes for whores. Christine de Pizan's 15th-century *Book of the Three Virtues* advises not only lady bosses, merchant women, and craftswomen. Christine also has good advice for the prostitutes who in their profession suffer bad nights and blows. If the woman of light morals wants to flee her work she can do it. But the perils of the business make escape difficult. If the whore wishes to stop enduring the baseness of those men who beat her, drag her about, threaten, and daily endanger her, then certainly she can escape. Christine reminds her readers that various blessed prostitute saints successfully repented their frivolous lives.

The prostitute must guard against the usual three things that may discourage her from reforming. First, the dishonest people she frequents will not permit it. Second, the world will scorn her. Third, she will have nothing to live on because she has no other craft.

Christine presents a remedy for all three problems, suggesting that a good whore can repent and never backslide, and, with God's protection, good people will welcome her because she has exchanged shame for honor. For gainful employment, Christine de Pizan suggests the courtesan try working in the laundry of a great house, or spinning, or caring for pregnant women, or tending the sick. If careful to dress modestly so to not attract men, she will maintain her virtue and earn her living. She will gain more profit from one cent honestly earned than one hundred gained in sin.

Prostitution waxed and waned in the Middle Ages for reasons never satisfactorily explained. Moral fashions notwithstanding, the major impetus for dramatic increases in prostitution at certain periods in particular countries may have depended upon economic competition with men.

At specific times women not only dominated crafts such as weaving silk and wool, but completely monopolized them. We can look for patterns in the laws. When do men and women voice the same complaints and enjoy the same prerogatives? When do craftswomen and craftsmen coexist peacefully, with competition between professional talent and training more pertinent than sex? When do women complain about craftsmen as opposed to craft malefactors? When do men complain about craftswomen as opposed to craft malefactors? When do citizens or craft guilds encourage government to regulate the trade so as to limit competition and increase privilege and profit? When does prostitution wax and when does prostitution wane?

In a local world peaceful and rich enough for people to spend money on more than mere subsistence, men and women trade value for value, creating enough work for every willing craftsman and craftswoman. Legislation controls excellence of the trade rather than access to the trade. Craftswomen and craftsmen coexist creatively. In some crafts, such as silkweaving in France, women hold dominion because of excellence.

In a local world where men are away at war or holy crusade, women work at all trades, professions, and crafts because they must. They must support themselves and their families, and they must advance the war economy with their production. Craftswomen come into preeminence when they are necessary as well as when they are good. With the men away fighting for country or for God, craftswomen thrive and dominate the crafts.

But after wars and crusades, men returning to their towns complain that women are stealing their work. They have risked limb and life and need to work but "their" jobs are now "gone," their markets are guarded by women, their work is women's work. Returning men, whether booty-laden or disappointment-bowed, are jealous of craftswomen's work.

Craftsmen now face business competition they cannot easily overcome by reason and by market methods, such as making a better product faster or cheaper. Craftsmen overcome competition by craftswomen by the easier, cheaper, effective conjunction between emotion and entitlement by need. "We suffered," the men say, and they did. "We are entitled," the men say. Now women are forced out of their jobs, sometimes forbidden to practice their crafts at all.

Prostitution in towns and cities seems dramatically to increase when returning soldiers bring home a flexible "foreign" morality, and bring home their now idle hands needing work. This the laws rehearse in their preambles preceding the exclusion of women from specific trades.

Some craftswomen suddenly unemployed, expecting and requiring paychecks to support their families, turn to whoring. Prostitution is one craft in which there is little to no competition from men; there is little fluctuation on price of raw materials to reduce the profit; there is great, renewable, nearly perpetual demand for services from an undiminishing clientele, which may require more service as it ages and increasingly has the money to buy it. A skilled and experienced woman is guaranteed an annual wage.

A vigorous complaint in 1461 suggests the way women who had dominated the cloth production of Bristol, England, suddenly disappeared from the industry. Returning soldiers, through the legislators, accused the weavers of Bristol of hiring women "by the which many and diverse of the king's liege people, likely men to do the king's service in his wars and defense of this land, sufficiently learned in the said [weaving] crafts, go vagrant and unoccupied and may not have their labor to their living." Bristol's weavers thereafter were forbidden to employ women.

MURDERERS

To Eleanor's house
Some go straight thither,
Be it slaty or slither:

Some, loath to be espied,
Start in at the back-side
Over the hedge and pale,
And all for the good ale.
Some had killed a man.
Catch them if you can.

Among the female felons of the 14th century were many murderers. Violent attacks causing death are rarer among medieval criminal women than men. Nevertheless, murderesses capably, successfully practiced their violent craft either for cash and goods, or for spite and vengeance. Medieval women murderers used swords and bludgeons, just as their male counterparts did. Female felons' common weapons appear to be the knife and the hatchet.

Some women murderers, like medieval men felons, were felony murderers who killed while robbing or stealing or assaulting or burning buildings by arson. Other women were domestic killers who eliminated members of their own families. For both professional and domestic murderers, killing methods were similar.

Poison was popular. Drowning was useful for dispatching an unwanted child, lover, or husband. Court records such as England's Justice Itinerant documents for the years 1300 through 1348 provide abundant examples, such as Alice Grut and Alice Grym, who drowned a three-day-old child in a river, with the full consent and connivance of three onlookers.

Knives and hatchets murdered both women and men. Sometimes the eternal domestic triangle of husband, wife, and lover neatly was straightened by the wife and lover joining forces to eliminate the superfluous husband. Robert Cullingworth and Thomas Daryl in 14th-century England both met their deaths thanks to such efficient pairing of talents.

Yet other women managed to dispatch husbands without the aid of collaborators. An intriguing court case preserves the testimony of a woman who killed her husband as he lay in bed. She claimed in court that her husband had suffered a fit of insanity and that she believed he had been "seized by Death." However, apparently doubting Death's efficiency, she decided to help. She cut her husband's throat with a small scythe and broke his skull with a bill hook.

Homicide within the family more frequently was directed against husbands than children, but infanticide may have occurred frequently. Though actual law court cases are few, nevertheless a certain strangeness in the data regarding male versus female children suggests that human intervention aided fate in eliminating unwanted babies, particularly girl-children. Child killing easily could be disguised as family accident: an inadvertent smothering, an accidental fall, a lamentable unintentional drowning. More murders probably went unrecorded than reached court dockets.

Among those women brought to trial for child murder, almost invariably the defense was insanity. Agnes Moyses killed her young son Adam during one of her frequent bouts of insanity. The widow Matilde of Buthanwell first tried suicide. Failing that, she returned to murder the children. But Marjorie Calvat sadistically, repeatedly knifed her two-year-old daughter to death, then forced her four-year-old child to roast to death in the flames of their hearth. These "insane" child killers were amateurs, demented women killing for some personal expiation, not for profit.

A rather different case was that of a well-known knight in Lincolnshire, Sir William Cantilupe, who was found dead in 1375 in a field near a highway. Elegantly dressed, wearing fine garments with spurs and a belt, he appeared to have been killed by highway robbers. But indictments ultimately were drawn against 12 members of his own household, including his wife Maude and her maid Agatha.

Apparently Maude and Agatha attacked Sir William violently while he slept in bed at night. His murderers then bathed his mortal wounds in water, put the naked body into a sack, and carried it for four miles. Carefully reclothing it, they threw the body into the field. Soon thereafter, Maude married Sir Thomas Kydale. He was under suspicion as having prompted the murder, and possibly as an accomplice to the crime.

Punishment for women murderers was essentially identical to that for men who killed intentionally. Brought to trial in identical fashion, men and female felons, if found guilty, were similarly hanged. Only treasonous acts, such as counterfeiting money or king-killing differentiated punishments sexually. The man convicted of treason was drawn and quartered. The treasonous woman was burned at the stake. Just as a man killing his overlord was guilty of treason, similarly a woman murdering her husband, her overlord, was cast to the flames.

Criminal women had yet another concession to their sex. If condemned to death, a woman could win a stay of execution due to pregnancy, for canon law prohibited killing a child in the womb. It was a defense frequently accomplished since most medieval jails had few indoor sports and were coeducational, men and women sharing cells.

Marjorie Berewick in 14th-century England was scheduled to die for having broken into the house of a prominent gentleman. She pleaded pregnancy. Her condition was examined, then affirmed, by the special jury of prison matrons appointed to investigate her claim. She was allowed to live until her child was born.

Felon Matilda Hereward managed to remain consistently pregnant from June 1301 through January 1303. Though she and her husband were condemned to die on the gallows on June 21, 1301, only her husband then was hanged. Matilda kept herself constantly with child, returning to jail to await each successive baby's birth. The jury and the justices in Northamptonshire found her pregnant in June 1301, September 1301, January 1302, June 1302, October 1302, and January 1303, a prodigious fecundity for new life to extend the life of one who had violated civil life.

THIEVES AND MARKET LAWBREAKERS

Instead of coin and money
Some bring Eleanor a coney,
And some a pot of honey,
Some salt, and some a spoon,
Some their hose, and some their shoon;
Thieves do bring
A harvest girdle, a wedding ring,
One brings her husband's hood
Because the ale is good;
Another brought her his cap
To offer to the ale-tap.

A baker convicted of fraud for selling underweight bread is punished by being carried through the town ignominiously tied to a
horse-drawn punishment cart called a hurdle. His deceitful bread
loaf is tied abound his neck as a necklace of shame. Women and
men were sentenced to the pillory, the women to the thewe, and the
hurdle if they were accused and convicted of violating regulations
on time of selling, place of sale, methods of weighing, purity of
ingredients, and freshness of product. Special courts had jurisdiction over specific market crimes. London's Assize of Ale handled
regulation of brewers and brewsters, the Assize of Bread controlled
bakers and baxters.

Women stole food, produce, possessions, and valuables, usually for profit.
Sometimes they could claim extenuating circumstances, such as starving
children whose need forced the mother to steal grain, bread, or vegetables.
But most court-recorded women thieves had professional appreciation for
their craft. They were interested in money, valuables, and the wanton
pleasures of brigandry.

Alice Garlic of Great Houghton apparently enjoyed robbing men. She stripped off their clothes, leaving them bare and taking all goods from them. She was brought to court for robbing three different men in precisely the same fashion.

Working alone or with accomplices as market profiteers, housebreakers, night-walking pickpockets, or highway robbers, women sold their goods to receivers or fences, many of whom were women. Some female fences received goods from their close relatives, sisters, daughters, husbands, or sons.

Ingenious petty larcenies in the marketplace combined illicit with licit craft. Women bakers often practiced a surprisingly lucrative type of dough stealing. Professional bakers used a long, flat kneading table called a molding board to shape dough into loaves before baking. Patrons would bring their unbaked dough to the bakeries for the final cooking, placing their raw loaves upon the molding board, traditionally fitted with a curtain or skirt at its front. The woman baker would then give that dough a final shaping.

Unknown to the patron, under the molding board a hidden servant would open a small trap door beneath the loaf, scrape out as much dough as he could manage without endangering the shape of the bread, and the baker then would place the now diminished dough in the oven for baking. The baker then used the reserved pilfered dough to make new breads for sale.

Ale makers, required to sell specific quantities of brew for set prices, found clever ways to alter their measuring cups. Since cups, pottles, half-quarts, and quarts were standard measures according to town or country regulation, the alewife desiring to shortchange her customers might follow the example of the 14th-century Londoner Alice de Caustone. She thickened the bottom of her ale measure, thereby building up the interior margins so its capacity was reduced by nearly one-third. In a Latin document dated 1364, Alice acknowledges that she has sold ale in a non-standard quart measure filled with one and one half inches of pitch, judiciously covered over with rosemary. Assayed by the standard of London, six of Alice's quarts would not make one proper gallon of ale.

For this falsehood and deceit, Alice was condemned to the pillory for women, the *thewe*. A public shaming device for criminals and accused malefactors, the woman's pillory either bound her head and hands to a pole or thrust them through boards cut to fit and restrain them. Punishments lasting hours or days exposed the offender to weather, ridicule, and attack. Alice's false measure was cut in two, with one half tied to the pillory, the other remaining in the chamber of the guildhall.

Around the same time, Marjorie Hore, fishwife, appeared before the mayor and aldermen of London with certain fish called soles, stinking, rotten, and unwholesome for human consumption. These she had displayed for sale "in deceit of the common people and against the ordinance." Since Marjorie did not deny these accusations, she was placed on the *thewe* for her fraud. The fish were burned.

Outside the markets, women thieves worked in pairs with either a female or male accomplice. Some joined roving bands or gangs. According to the court documents of the 14th-century English manor of Wakefield, Alice Wakefeud was indicted for larceny with an accomplice named Nicholas, the parish chaplain. Alice and Nicholas had absconded at night with assets belonging to her husband: money from his purse, three gold rings worth eighteen pence, a fine drinking vessel called a mazer valued at twelve pence, a napkin, a towel, a gown, a new hood taken from her husband's pack, as well as many other valuable objects. After riding to Aylisbury on Nicholas's horse, the pair sold the goods there. Alice pocketed the sales money and quietly returned to her husband.

BEGGARS, GOSSIPS, AND SCOLDS

Then thither came drunken Alice
And she was full of tales
Of tidings in Wales
And of the Portingales,
With "Lo, gossip, ywis,
Thus and thus it is."

She speaks thus in her hood,
She pissed where she stood
Then began to weep,
And forthwith fell asleep.

The gossip, the beggar, and the scold also frequented Eleanor's imagined tavern.

Alice de Salasbury, a 14th-century beggar, was forced to the *thewe* for having taken the little daughter of a London grocer and carried her away, stripping her of clothes so that she might not be recognized by her family, in order to go begging with Alice and thereby increase her gain.

Evil-talking, backbiting, shrewish women could be condemned to the *thewe* for being common scolds. Alice Shether was indicted in London in 1375 as a scold. All her neighbors complained that they were afflicted by her malicious words and abuse. She sowed envy among them, discord, and ill will, repeatedly defaming, molesting, and backbiting many of them, sparing neither rich nor poor. Scolding damaged neighbors and violated the ordinance of the city, and the jury judged her guilty. Scolds and slanderers feloniously using the armed tongue were compelled to wear a head armor that forcibly closed the mouth, allowing for breathing and seeing but adorning the head with asses' ears.

WITCHES

Female felons often united sexuality with their crimes. The whore, the thief, the murderer, and the witch practicing their trades either directly exercised their own genitalia or manipulated men's desires and fears. Remarkably, the achievements of women in the illicit trades converged with the excellences of women physicians. Witchcraft was their common business.

Opposite: Using unnatural raw ingredients such as human flesh, and magical cooking methods such as instant fireless heat, witches create an unholy sabbath meal. Witches' brews were thought to be perversions and inversions of pious Christian table manners. Food expressed spirituality, and eating habits exemplified a person's virtue or vice. Gula or Gluttony was thought to be the seducing sin that corrupted the world. While Pride was the deadliest sin, Gluttony was the first sin: Just as Adam ate his way out of Paradise, so man eats his way into sin. This sin tempts daily, is easy to commit, and is hard to forgive. St. Thomas Aquinas, St. Augustine, St. Paul, St. Gregory, interpreters such as Peraldus, Pennaforte, and even Chaucer's Pardoner connect the throat and stomach to the soul. Chaucer's Parson, following St. Thomas Aquinas, explains that the person succumbing to gluttony cannot withstand other sins. Magic rituals of eating, transformations of common foods into something other than what they seem, foods as proof of supernatural power, ritual food offerings to God, eucharistic transubstantiation of wine and bread into the blood and body of Christ all ally food with the spiritual condition. While noblewomen cultivated tastes and appetites as proof of education, political power, and economic supremacy, Christian moralists saw in elaborate foods and eating ceremonials the devil's method of acquiring converts. Witches' sabbath feasts were thought to praise and propitiate Satan. The Devil further empowered his disciples who, having tasted sin, were energized by the food of demonic love.

The lady doctor there
Certainly could swear.
She seemed to be a leech
And began to preach
Of the virtue of an unset leek,
And of her husband's breach.
And with good ale barm
She could make a charm
To help with-all a stitch.
She seemed to be a witch.

Though medical practitioners often were hauled to court for malpractice, a medieval woman physician named Marjorie Hales of Worcester, England, in 1302 was accused of malpractice in an especially pernicious fashion: Roger Aldrich threw her into a river. Ostensibly, she had unsuccessfully treated Roger or a member of his family. Marjorie herself raised the hue and cry, and the court subsequently found Roger guilty of assault. Why this water attack?

Roger was attempting to learn whether Marjorie was a witch. The water ordeal was a common medieval test for ascertaining sorcery or witchcraft. Depending upon the country or year, if the submerged witch sank, that was proof she was weighted down by her demons drawing her back to Hell. In other places and times, if she floated and swam, that was proof that evil spirits of the air buoyed her against the body's natural tendency to submerge. Either way, she whom the test determined was a witch then was burned at the stake.

Magic and witchcraft explained otherwise inexplicable successes and failures. Eleanor Cobham, duchess of Gloucester, was forced to endure a long, painful penance in 1441 for having procured a prognosticator to predict by magical means the death of King Henry VI. Jacquetta of Luxemburg, the ex-Duchess of Bedford, was accused of interfering by witchcraft in the sex life of Edward IV. She magically inspired his infatuation for the lovely Elizabeth Wydville, inciting his lascivious desires by her sorcery. Such noble, wealthy women underwent an ordeal (by water, burning coals, shards of glass) to prove their innocence or guilt. Death by burning was customary punishment for conviction of witchcraft.

Lower-class women, as well as some men, were punished at the pillory for practicing magic. But magic easily slid into witchery. Both magicians and witches used divination to foretell the future. A clever diviner consulting bowls of water, crystal globes, balls of clay, animal innards, elaborate breads, hand lines (chiromancy), or forehead wrinkles (metoposcopy), could predict reality. Witches, however, possessing more than foreknowledge, exercised power and dominion. Witches capable of foretelling the future also could affect it malevolently, causing distress, disaster, and death.

Women doctors, women pharmacists, and other female medical personnel were often accused of witchcraft. Women practitioners effecting miraculous cures were thought not saints but witches. Their medical successes were ascribed not to divine but diabolic influence. When the woman physician's hands of healing were thought to have touched the Devil's genitalia they were roughly tied behind her back before she was offered up burnt to heaven.

Once the epidemic of witch burning abated, few women medical practitioners had survived the fever. The dramatic decline in the number of women practicing medicine corresponds remarkably with the intense increase in witch trials, ordeals, and immolations, seemingly assuring the disappearance of the medical textbooks and records of women doctors such as Trotula of Salerno, Hildegard of Bingen, and other women practitioners of ophthalmology, obstetrics, orthopedics, and surgery.

Medieval Christian condemnation of witchcraft was stimulated by a misogyny different from the earlier heritages of women in the illicit trades in classical Greece, Rome, and Judaism. Medieval inquisitors hated witches with a passion traceable to scholasticism's otherwise admirable attempt to understand the natural world rationally. How could men pledged to celibacy rationally and naturally shun women? How could logic promote the voluntary separation of the sexes? How could the unattainable desirable be repulsed as repugnant?

Inquisitors cleverly subverted law and science, creating a chain of spurious knowledge with early links to Aristotle, natural philosophers, later physicians, and philosophers such as Albertus Magnus and his disciple,

The woman whose only interest is her own reflection becomes consort of the Devil. Pseudo-scientific texts such as Malleus
Malleficarum (The Hammer of Witches), by 15th-century
Dominican Inquisitors Heinrich Kramer and Jacob Sprenger,
claimed that women witches have had sexual relations with demons,
knowing and loving demonic anatomy. Here a naked devil expos-
es his anus and tail to the vain woman who sees it reflected in her
mirror. This illustrates the medieval adage: "The woman who loves
her own mirror loves only the vile devil's ass."

WOMEN AT WORK IN MEDIEVAL EUROPE
126

the so-called Pseudo-Albertus Magnus, who wrote the immensely influential book called *Women's Secrets (De Secretis Mulierum)*.

Pseudo-Albertus was a cleric addressing other celibate men. He exaggerated and perverted benign physiological processes, customary midwifery, and prostitution to justify the malevolent persecution of women, especially old women and medical women. His book quivers with a celibate clergy's fear of sexuality, menstruation, conception, abortion, and the unknown. Thirteen chapters of *Women's Secrets* concern the generation of the embryo, the formation of the fetus, the influence of the planets, teratology, monsters in nature, the birthing of the fetus from the uterus, signs of conception, pre-birth sexual determination, indicators of "corruption of virginity," "signs of chastity," womb defects, impediments to conception, and sperm generation.

Throughout this powerful, pernicious text, women's bodies, their sexuality, and their temperaments are depicted as naturally polluting and destructive. If science defined women as naturally corrupt and corrupting, logic required their avoidance, possibly their persecution, and, often, their execution.

Pseudo-Albertus directly influenced popular 15th-century inquisitorial treatises on witchcraft, witches, and female criminal behavior, such as *The Hammer of Witches (Malleus Maleficarum)*. Kramer and Sprenger, the Dominican inquisitor-writers of *The Hammer,* forged another strong link in the chain of misogynist ideology. Women are prone to witchcraft, they posited. For this crime, they deserve death.

Kramer and Sprenger wrote that women's sexuality turns men's minds from good and seduces them to sin. Women's criminal proclivities are natural. Daughters of Eve are born to deceit and lies. Women's inherited criminal leanings derive, according to the *Hammer of Witches,* from "a defect in the formation of the first woman since she was formed from a bent rib, that is a rib from the breast, which is bent, as it were, in a contrary direction to a man. And since, through this defect, she is an imperfect animal, she always deceives."

The virulence of such misogyny indirectly testifies to the power of women in the illicit trades in medieval daily life. Proud prostitutes, clever murderers, thieves, arsonists, ingenious market cheats, and petty larcenists were known in their own time by their illegal, bold works. By their work, they merit celebration now.

Just as women physicians, artists, websters, brewsters, mineral miners, wool merchants, abbesses, and landed leaders thrived in the world of labor, so women notorious in the underworld thrived as prostitutes, thieves, and felons. All these productive women in western Europe between the 10th and 15th centuries in England, France, Spain, Germany, Italy, Poland, and Hungary enable us today to appreciate the sexual balance in medieval society and the important history of women at work. Medieval life was not entirely dominated by men. Medieval splendor was not created by men alone.

NOTES AND
REFERENCES

Each of the five chapters of *Women at Work in Medieval Europe* has its own notes and references. For each chapter, the first list of books treats the general subject. Specific topics follow with relevant references. Each topic appears in the order in which it appears in the text, under the relevant subheading. Each subheading appears in **boldface** type.

There are no footnote or endnote numbers in the text. Each topic under each subheading has a logical identifier phrase keyed to the text. The identifier phrase, beginning in the word *on,* is printed in capital letters preceding the detailed references.

Archival and primary sources precede analytical and secondary sources. Last names precede first names, as in a customary bibliography.

For four decades encountering documents of medieval women at work, I have gathered information in libraries, museums, universities, courthouses, guildhalls, public record offices, and private collections in America, France, Germany, Italy, Spain, Israel, Australia, South Africa, and England. At almost every juncture, some aspect of medical law was more important to me than gender of the protagonist. Usually I was startled the women were there.

As an attorney specializing in medical law, and having written about medical malpractice history since the 1960s, I never intentionally sought out women medical practitioners or malpractitioners. But their remarkable prevalence in law court records enabled me to prove that women physicians and surgeons were so common that laws distinguished doctors who were men from doctors who were women, held them to the same professional standards, and similarly punished their infractions.

My discovery of certain women at work often was accidental. In London, for instance, my research on medico-legal questions only tangentially related to other crimes and punishments. I read legal documents dating from the 12th through the 15th centuries written in Latin, Norman French, and various Middle English dialects, including the stunning legal miscellanies preserved in the London Public Record Office in binders labeled alphabetically "Letter Book A" through "Letter Book I." I also consulted land transfer contracts, wills, coroners' rolls, jail delivery rolls for royal circuit courts, eyre rolls with their fascinating jury questions called "articles of the eyre," king's bench rolls, chancery proceedings, manor court rolls, calendar rolls, close rolls, patent rolls, and assize rolls.

Near documents of critical medico-legal interest I recorded documents of more general felonious import, such as a Latin court record of a 14th-century trial during the reign of King Edward III for theft and the punishment by hanging of a woman thief named Desiderata de Toryntone. She had stolen 30 dishes and 24 saltcellars and was apprehended red-handed, with 14 dishes and 12 salts on her person. I found this in Letter Book E, dated 1337. Therefore, in the fifth section dedicated to women in the illicit trades, I tell you about Desiderata and refer you as well to superb studies of women criminals in medieval Europe, especially England.

In notes for chapter 4 on market women and craftswomen, I note court cases where the malefactor's danger to the populace was less to its health than to its commerce. Among women and men frauds in 14th-century London were "hucksters" or retailers using a false measure called a *chopyn*. During the reign of King Edward III, Alice Hurle, Agnes Damas, Johanna Hanel, Cristina atte Felde, Elena, Cecily, and others were convicted of using the *chopyn* to the detriment of the populace and punished. For the precise 14th-century reference in the

London archives and for interpretive analyses of market larcenies, I offer:

Letter Book G, Folio 258 (1370).

Cosman, Madeleine Pelner. "A Chicken for Chaucer's Kitchen." In *Fabulous Feasts: Medieval Cookery and Ceremony.* New York, 1976, 1978, 1998.

Chapter 1
WOMEN WRITERS AND POETS

ON WOMEN WRITERS AND
WOMEN LITERARY PATRONS:

Barratt, Alexandra. *Women's Writing in Middle English.* London, New York, 1992.

Berman, Constance, and Charles Connell. *The Worlds of Medieval Women: Creativity, Influence, Imagination.* Morgantown, 1985.

Bornstein, Diane. *Mirrors of Courtesy.* Hamden, Conn., 1975.

Bornstein, Diane, ed. *Ideals for Women in the Works of Christine de Pizan.* Michigan, 1981.

Cherewatuk, Karen, and Ulrike Wiethaus. *Dear Sister: Medieval Women and the Epistolary Genre.* Philadelphia, 1993.

Droke, Peter. *Women Writers of the Middle Ages.* New York, 1984.

Duckett, Eleanor. *Women and Their Letters in the Early Middle Ages.* Northampton, 1964.

Ferrante, Joan M. *To the Glory of Her Sex: Women's Roles in the Composition of Medieval Texts.* Bloomington, 1997.

———. *Woman as Image in Medieval Literature.* New York, 1976.

Ferrier, Janet. *Forerunners of the French Novel: an Essay on the Development of the Novella in the Late Middle Ages.* London, 1954.

Hentsch, Alice A. *De la littérature didactique du moyen age s'adressant spécialement aux femmes.* Geneva, 1975.

Holloway, Julia B., Constance S. Wright, and Joan Bechtold. *Equally in God's Image: Women in the Middle Ages.* New York, 1990.

Kemp-Welch, Alice. *Of Six Medieval Women.* London, 1913.

King, Margaret L., and Albert Rabil, Jr. *Her Immaculate Hand: Selected Works by and about the Women Humanists of Quattrocento Italy.* Binghamton, 1992, 1997.

Lucas, Angela. *Women in the Middle Ages: Religion, Marriage, and Letters.* New York, 1983.

McCash, June Hall. *The Cultural Patronage of Medieval Women.* Athens, Georgia, 1996.

Meale, Carol. *Women and Literature in Britain, 1150–1500*. Cambridge, New York, 1993.

Meiss, Millard. *French Painting in the Time of Jean, Duc de Berry.* London, 1967.

Morewedge, Rosmarie Thee, ed. *The Role of Woman in the Middle Ages.* Albany, 1975.

Pernoud, Regine. *Blanche of Castille.* New York, 1975.

Russell, Rinaldin. *Italian Women Writers: a Bio-Bibliographical Source Book.* Westport, 1994.

Solente, S. *Le Livre de la Mutaçion de Fortune, par Christine de Pisan.* Paris, 1959–1968.

Solterer, Helen. *The Master and Minerva: Disputing Women in French Medieval Culture.* Berkeley, 1995.

Surtz, Ronald. *Writing Women in Late and Early Modern Spain.* Philadelphia, 1995.

Vetere, Benedetto, and Paolo Renzi, eds. *Profili di donne.* Galatina, 1986.

Willard, Charity Cannon. *Development of the Novella in the Late Middle Ages.* London, 1954.

———. "A Fifteenth-Century View of Women's Role in Medieval Society." In *The Role of Woman in the Middle Ages,* edited by Rosemarie Morewedge. Albany, 1975.

———. *The Livre de la Paix of Christine de Pisan.* 'S Gravenhage, 1958.

Willard, Charity Cannon and Madeleine Pelner Cosman. *Medieval Woman's Mirror of Honor: The Treasury of the City of Ladies by Christine de Pizan,* translation of and introduction to *The Book of Three Virtues.* New York, 1989.

Wilson, Katharina. *Medieval Women Writers.* Athens, Georgia, 1984.

TROUBADOURS

ON WOMEN AND MEN TROUBADOURS:

Bogin, Meg. *The Women Troubadours.* New York, 1976.

Briffault, Robert. *The Troubadours.* Bloomington, 1965.

Goldin, Frederick. *Lyrics of the Troubadours and the Trouveres.* New York, 1963.

Nelli, René. *L'Erotique des troubadours.* Toulouse, 1963.

ON COURTLY LOVE:

Andreas Capellanus. *The Art of Courtly Love.* Translated and edited by J. J. Parry. New York, 1941.

Bloch, Howard. *Medieval Misogyny and the Invention of Western Romantic Love.* Chicago, 1991.

Dronke, Peter. *Medieval Latin and the Rise of the European Love Lyric.* Oxford, 1968.

Duby, Georges. *Medieval Marriage.* Translated by Elborg Forster. Baltimore, 1978.

Ferrante, Joan, and George Economou, eds. *In Pursuit of Perfection: Courtly Love in Medieval Literature.* Port Washington, 1975.

Lewis, C. S. *The Allegory of Love.* Oxford, 1970.

Lochrie, Karma. *Covert Operations: The Medieval Uses of Secrecy.* Philadelphia, 1999.

Moller, Herbert. "The Social Causation of the Courtly Love Complex," *Comparative Studies in Society and History* 1 (1958): 147–163.

Oppenheimer, Paul. *Birth of the Modern Mind.* Oxford, 1989.

Wack, Mary. *Lovesickness in the Middle Ages: The Viaticum and Its Commentaries.* Philadelphia, 1990.

MARIE DE FRANCE

ON MARIE DE FRANCE'S LAIS AND OTHER WORKS:

Marie de France. *Fables.* Translated by Harriet Spiegel. Toronto, 1987.

———. *French Medieval Romances.* Translated by Eugene Mason. London, 1932.

———. *Graelent and Guingamor: Two Breton Lays.* Edited and translated by Russell Weingartner. New York, 1985.

———. *Lais.* Translated by Robert Hanning & Joan Ferrante. New York, 1978.

———. *Les lais.* Edited by Jean Rychner. Paris, 1966.

———. *The Lais of Marie de France.* Translated by Glyn S. Burgess and Keith Busby. Harmondsworth, 1986.

———. *Lais. Proud Knight, Fair Lady: The Twelve Lais of Marie de France.* Translated by Naomi Lewis. New York, 1989.

———. *Lays.* Translated by Eugene Mason. New York, 1959.

———. *Medieval Fables.* Translated by Jeanette Beer. New York, 1983.

Bayrav, Seuheylaa. *Symbolisme médiéval: Béroul, Marie, Chrétien.* Paris, 1957.

Berechiah ha-Nakdan. *Fables of a Jewish Aesop.* Translated by Moses Hadas; introduction by W. T. H. Jackson, New York, 1967.

Burgess, Glyn S. *The Lais of Marie de France: Text and Context.* Athens, Georgia, 1987.

Cook, Robert, and Mattias Tveitane. *Strengleikar: An Old Norse Translation of Twenty-One Old French Lais.* Oslo, 1979.

Duckett, Eleanor. *Women and Their Letters in the Early Middle Ages.* Northampton, 1964.

Ferrante, Joan. *Woman as Image in Medieval Literature.* New York, 1976.

———. *To the Glory of Her Sex: Women's Roles in the Composition of Medieval Texts.* Bloomington, 1997.

Ferrier, Janet. *Forerunners of the French Novel: An Essay on the Development of the Novella in the Late Middle Ages.* London, 1954.

Hentsch, Alice A. *De la littérature didactique du moyen age s'adressant spécialement aux femmes.* Geneva, 1975.

Reeves, James. *The Shadow of the Hawk, and Other Stories by Marie de France.* New York, 1977.

Marie de France's work was imitated in 12th-century Hebrew literature. Of her beast fables, 37 are also found in the fables of the Jewish Aesop,

Berechiah ha-Nakdan. Another 13 animal fables apparently are shared only by the Jewish fabulist and Marie de France and unknown to Latin, Greek, or other contemporary medieval literary collections.

ON FABLIAUX, RIBALD HUMOR, AND THE EARLY NOVEL:

Benson, Larry D., and Theodor M. Andersson, eds. *The Literary Context of Chaucer's Fabliaux*. Indianapolis and New York, 1971.

Cholakian, P., and B. Cholakian. *The Early French Novella*. Albany, 1974.

Feral, Edmond. *Les Jongleurs en France au moyen age*. Paris, 1910.

Ferrier, Janet. *Forerunners of the French Novel: An Essay on the Development of the Novella in the Late Middle Ages*. London, 1954.

Harrison, Robert. *Gallic Salt*. Berkeley, 1974.

Hart, W. M. "The Narrative Art of the Old French Fabliau." In *Anniversary Papers . . . G. L. Kittredge*. Boston, 1913. Reprint. New York, 1967.

Hellman, Robert, and Richard O'Gorman. *Fabliaux: Ribald Tales from the Old French*. New York, 1965.

Johnston, R. C. and D. D. Owen. *Fabliaux*. Oxford, 1965.

Nykrog, Per. *Les Fabliaux*. Copenhagen, 1957.

Regalado, Nancy. *Poetic Patterns in Rutebeuf*. New Haven, 1970.

Valentini, Giuseppe. *Les Fabliaux de l'Espace*. Naples, 1965.

ON MÄRCHEN AND FOLK MOTIFS:

Stith Thompson. *Motif-Index of Folk-Literature: A Classification of Narrative Elements in Folktale . . . Medieval Romances . . . Fabliaux*. Bloomington, 1932–36; computer file, CD-ROM, Bloomington, 1993.

CHRISTINE DE PIZAN

ON CHRISTINE DE PIZAN:

Because Christine de Pizan was so prolific and now so justly popular, here are (1) translations, (2) modern editions of her writings, and (3) background studies and textual analyses of her books. With Professor Charity Cannon Willard, I shared the joy of translating Christine de Pizan's instruction book for women in power called *The Book of the Three Virtues or The Treasury of the City of Ladies,* published in 1989.

1. TRANSLATIONS OF CHRISTINE DE PIZAN'S WRITINGS

Christine de Pizan. *The Boke of the Cyte of Ladyes*. Translated by Brian Anslay. London, 1521. Reprinted in *Distaves and Dames: Renaissance Treatises for and about Women,* edited by Diane Bornstein. Delmar, N. Y., 1978.

———. *The Book of the City of Ladies.* Translated by Earl Jeffrey Richards. New York, 1982.

———. *The Book of the Duke of True Lovers,* Translated by Alice Kemp-Welch; ballads, translated by Lawrence Binyon and Eric D. Maclagen. London, 1908.

———. *The Book of Fayttes of Arms and of Chyvalrye*: Translated and printed by William Caxton from the French by Christine de Pizan, edited by A. T. P. Byles. London, 1932, 1937.

———. *The Book of the Three Virtues or the Treasury of the City of Ladies.* Translated by Charity Cannon Willard and Madeleine Pelner Cosman. Published as *A Medieval Woman's Mirror of Honor: The Treasury of the City of Ladies by Christine de Pizan.* New York, 1989.

———. *Das Buch von den Drei Tugenden in Portugiescher Ubersetzung.* Edited by Dorotee Carstens-Grokenberger. Munster, 1961.

———. *La Ditie de Jeanne d'Arc.* Edited and translated by Angus J. Kennedy and Kenneth Varty. Oxford, 1977.

———. *The Fayt of Arms and of Chyvalrie, Facsimile of Caxton's 1489 edition.* Amsterdam, New York, 1968.

———. *The Epistle of Othia.* Translated by Sir Stephen Scrope; edited by Curt F. Buhler. London, 1970.

———. *The Epistle of Othia to Hector.* Translated by Anthony Babington; edited by James D. Gordon. Philadelphia, 1942.

———. *The Epistle of the Prison of Human Life.* Translated by Josette Wisman. New York, 1985.

———. *O Espelho de Cristina.* Edited by Maria Manuela de Silva Nunes Ribeiro Cruzeiro. Lisbon, 1965.

———. "The Letter of Cupid." In *Hoccleve's Works: The Minor Poems,* edited by I. Gollancz. London, 1925.

———. *The Letter of Cupid in the Bannatyne Manuscript.* Edited by W. Todd Ritchie. Edinburgh and London, 1930.

———. *The Middle English Translation of Christine de Pisan's Livre du Corps de Policie.* Edited by Diane Bornstein. Heidelberg, 1977.

———. *Morale Proverbes of Chrystine.* Facsimile of Caxton's 1478 Edition. Translated by Anthony Woodville. Amsterdam, New York, 1970.

———. *La Querelle de la Rose: Letters and Documents.* Edited by Joseph L. Baird and John Kane. Chapel Hill, 1978.

———. *The Treasure of the City of Ladies.* Translated by Sara Lawson. London, 1985.

2. MODERN EDITIONS OF CHRISTINE DE PIZAN'S WORKS

Christine de Pizan. *L'Avision de Christine.* Edited by Sister Mary Louise Towner. Washington, 1932.

———. *Ballades, Rondeaux, and Virelais.* Edited by Kenneth Varty. Leicester, 1965.

———. *Cent Ballades d'Amant et de Dame.* Edited by Jacqueline Cerquiglini. Paris, 1982.

———. *Le debat sur le Roman de la Rose.* Edited and translated by Eric Hicks. Paris, 1977.

———. *La Ditie de Jeanne d'Arc.* Edited by Angus J. Kennedy and Kenneth Varty. Oxford, 1977.

———. *Epistre de la prison de vie humaine.* Edited by Angus J. Kennedy. Glasgow, 1984.

———. *La Lamentation sur les maux de la France.* In *Melanges de Langue et Littérature Françaises du Moyen Age et de la Renaissance Offerts à Charles Foulon.* Edited by Angus J. Kennedy. Rennes, 1980.

———. *Lettre a Isabeau de Bavière. Anglo-Norman Letters and Petitions from All Souls Ms. 182.* Edited by M. Dominica Legge. Oxford, 1971.

———. *Le Livre du Chemin de Long Estude.* Edited by Robert Puschel. Berlin, 1881.

———. *Le Livre du Corps de Policie.* Edited by Robert H. Lucas. Geneva, 1967.

———. *Le Livre des Fais et Bonnes Meurs du Sage Roy Charles V.* Edited by Suzanne Solente. Paris, 1936–1941.

———. *Le Livre de la Mutation de Fortune.* Edited by Suzanne Solente. Paris, 1959–1966.

———. *Le Livre de la Paix.* Edited by Charity Cannon Willard. The Hague, 1958.

———. *Oeuvres.* Edited by Jeanine Moulin. Paris, 1962.

———. *Oeuvres Politiques.* Edited by Maurice Roy. Paris, 1886–1896.

———-. *Sept Psaumes Allegorises.* Edited by Ruth Ringland Rains. Washington, D.C., 1965.

3. CRITICAL, BIOGRAPHICAL, AND CONTEXTUAL STUDIES OF CHRISTINE

Boldingh-Goernans, W. L. *Christine de Pizan (1364–1430): Haar Tijd, Haar Leven, Haar Werken.* Rotterdam, 1948.

Bornstein, Diane. "The Ideal of the Lady of the Manor as Reflected in Christine de Pizan's Livre des Trois Vertus." In *Ideals for Women in the Works of Christine de Pizan,* edited by Diane Bornstein. Michigan, 1981.

Castel, Francoise du. *Ma Grand-mere Christine de Pizan.* Paris, 1936.

———. *Damoiselle Christine de Pizan.* Paris, 1973.

Cosman, Madeleine Pelner. "Christine de Pizan's Well-Tempered Feminism." *Helicon Nine: The Journal of Women's Arts and Letters* (1983). Republished in *The Helicon Nine Reader,* edited by Gloria Vando Hickok. Kansas City, 1990.

———. "A 15th-Century Women's Utopia." A review of *The City of Ladies,* translated by E. J. Richards. *New Directions for Women* (1983).

———. "Powerful Women of Royal Courts." A review of *A Woman's Life in the Court of the Sun King, Letters of Liselotte von der Pfalz,* by Elborg Forster, and *Christine de Pizan,* by Charity Cannon Willard. *New Directions for Women* (1985).

Dulac, Liliane, "Inspiration mystique et savoir politique: les conseils aux veuves chez Francesco da Barbarino et chez Christine de Pizan." In *Melanges a la Memoire de Franco Simone.* 113–141. Geneva, 1980.

Favier, Marguerite. *Christine de Pisan: Muse des Cours Souveraines.* Lausanne, 1967.

Figueiredo, A. J. de. "Espelho de Cristina." In *Revista Brasileira de Folologia* 3 (1957): 117–119.

Hindman, Sandra L. *Christine de Pizan's "Epistre d'Othea," Painting and Politics at the Court of Charles VI.* Toronto, 1988.

Jackson, W. T. H. *The Literature of the Middle Ages.* New York, 1960.

Kennedy, Angus J. *Christine de Pizan: A Bibliographical Guide.* London, 1984, 1994.

Ladourie, Emmanuel LeRoy. *Montaillou: The Promised Land of Error.* Translated by Barbara Bray. New York, 1978.

Laigle, Mathilde. *Le Livre des Trois Vertus de Christine de Pisan et son milieu historique et littéraire.* Paris, 1912.

McLeod, Enid. *The Order of the Rose: The Life and Ideals of Christine de Pizan.* London, Totowa, 1976.

Nicolson, Marjorie Hope. "The Discovery of Space." In *Medieval and Renaissance Studies.* Edited by O. B. Hardison. Chapel Hill, 1966.

Nys, Ernest. *Christine de Pisan et ses Principales Oeuvres.* Brussels, 1914.

Pernoud, Regine. *Christine de Pisan.* Paris, 1982.

Pinet, Marie-Josephe. *Christine de Pisan (1364–1430): Etude Biographique et Littéraire.* Paris, 1927.

Richards, Earl Jeffrey. "Christine de Pizan and the Question of Feminist Rhetoric." *Modern Language Association Conference* 22(1983): 15–24.

Solente, Suzanne. "Christine de Pizan." *L'Histoire littéraire de la France.* Vol. 40. Paris, 1969.

Willard, Charity Cannon. "Christine de Pizan's *Livre des Trois Vertus:* Feminine Ideal or Practical Advice?" In *Ideals for Women in the Works of Christine de Pizan,* edited by Diane Bornstein, 91–116. Michigan, 1981.

———. *Christine de Pizan:Her Life and Works.* New York, 1984.

———. "A Portuguese Translation of Christine de Pizan's Livre des Trois Vertus." *PMLA* 78 (1963): 459–464.

———. "The Manuscript Tradition of the Livre des Trois Vertus and Christine de Pizan's Audience." *Journal of the History of Ideas* 27 (1966): 433–444.

———. "A Fifteenth-Century View of Women's Role in Medieval Society: Christine de Pizan's Livre des Trois Vertus." In *The Role of Women in the Middle Ages,* edited by Rosalie T. Morewedge, 90–120. Albany, London, 1975.

Yenal, Edith. *Christine de Pisan: A Bibliography of Her Writings and About Her.* Metuchen and London, 1982.

MARGUERITE DE NAVARRE
ON MARGUERITE DE NAVARRE:
Marguerite de Navarre. *L'Heptameron.* Edited by Michel François. Paris, 1960.
———. *Nouvelles.* Edited by Yves Le Hir. Paris, 1967.

Delegue, Yves. "L'Heptameron est-il un anti-Bocace?" *Travaux de linguistique et de littérature 4:2.* Strassbourg, 1966.

Febvre, Lucien. *Autour de l'Heptameron.* Paris, 1941.

Gelernt, Jules. *World of Many Loves: The Heptameron of Marguerite de Navarre.* Chapel Hill, 1966.

Hartley, K. H. *Bandello and the Heptameron.* Melbourne, 1960.

Jourda, Pierre. *Marguerite d'Angoulême.* Paris 1930, 1966.

Kasprzyk, Krystyna. "La matière traditionnelle et sa fonction dans l'Heptameron." *Romanisches Yarhbuch* 18. Hamburg, 1967.

Keller, Abraham. *The Telling of Tales in Rabelais.* Frankfurt, 1963.

Lebegue, Raymond. "L'Heptameron: un attrape-mondains." In *Melanges Marcel Raymond.* London, 1967.

Saulnier, V. L. *Marguerite de Navarre: Théâtre profane.* Paris, 1946, 1963.

Telle, Emile. *L'Oeuvre de Marguerite d'Angoulême, reine de Navarre et la Querelle des Femmes.* Toulouse, 1937.

Tetel, Marcel. *Marguerite de Navarre's Heptameron.* Durham, 1973.

Chapter 2

MEDICAL WOMEN: PHYSICIANS, SURGEONS, AND PHARMACISTS

ON WOMEN PHYSICIANS AND SURGEONS, THEIR PRACTICES, AND MALPRACTICES:

Arano, Luisa C. *Medieval Health Handbook: Tacuinum Sanitatis.* Translated by Oscar Ratti and Adele Westbrook. New York, 1976.

Calendar of Plea and Memoranda Rolls of the City of London 1323–1364. Edited by R. R. Sharpe. London, 1899.

Calendar of Wills in the Court of Husting. Edited by R. R. Sharpe. London, 1899.

Campbell, A. *The Black Death and Men of Learning.* New York, 1931.

Chartularium universitatis Parisiensis. Edited by H. Denifle and E. Chatelain. Paris, 1889–97.

Cosman, Madeleine Pelner. "Fountain, River, Privy, Pot: Medieval London's Polluted Waters." In *Fabulous Feasts: Medieval Cookery and Ceremony.* New York, 1976.

———. "Malpractice and Peer Review in Medieval England." *Transactions of the American Academy of Ophthalmology and Otolaryngology* 80 (May–June 1975):293–297.

———. "Medical Fees, Fines, and Forfeits in Medieval England." *Man and Medicine* (1975): 133–58.

———. "Medieval Medical Malpractice and Chaucer's Physician." *New York State Journal of Medicine* 19 (1972): 2439–44.

———. "Medieval Medical Malpractice: The Dicta and the Dockets." *Bulletin of New York Academy of Medicine* 49 (1973): 22–47.

———. "Medieval Medical Nutrition." *Australian Journal of Food and Nutrition* 42 (1986): 100–104.

———. "Miniatures: Medieval Medicine in Art." A review of Peter Murray Jones's *Medieval Medical Miniatures. Journal of the American Medical Association,* February 1987.

Depouy, Edmond. *Medicine in the Middle Ages.* Translated by T. C. Minor. Cincinnati, 1889.

Forbes, T. R. *The Midwife and the Witch.* New Haven, 1966.

Fort, George. *Medical Economy During the Middle Ages.* New York, 1970.

Friedenwald, Harry. "Jewish Doctoresses in the Middle Ages." In *The Jews and Medicine.* New York, 1967.

Hamilton, George. "Trotula." *Modern Philology* 4 (1906): 377–380.

Hughes, M. *Women Healers in Medieval Life and Literature.* New York, 1943.

Issues of the Exchequer. Edited by F. Devon. London, 1937.

Kibre, Pearl. "The Faculty of Medicine at Paris, Charlatanism, and Unlicensed Medical Practices in the Later Middle Ages," In *Legacies in Law and Medicine,* edited by C. R. Burns. New York, 1977.

Kittredge, G. L. *Witchcraft in Old and New England.* Cambridge, 1929.

MacKinney, Loren. *Medical Illustrations in Medieval Manuscripts.* Berkeley and Los Angeles, 1965.

Marx, Alexander. "The Correspondence Between the Rabbis of Southern France and Maimonides about Astrology." *Hebrew Union College Annual* 3 (1926): 311–58.

Maubray, John. *The Female Physician.* London, 1724.

Mead, Kate Campbell-Hurd. *A History of Women in Medicine.* Boston, 1973.

Nicaise, E., ed. *La grande chirugurie de Guy de Chauliac.* Paris, 1890.

Noonan, J. T. *Contraception: A History of Its Treatment by the Catholic Theologians and Canonists.* Cambridge, 1966.

———. *The Morality of Abortion: Legal and Historical Perspectives.* Cambridge, Mass., 1970.

Packard, F. R. *History of the School of Salernum.* New York, 1920.

Power, Eileen, "Some Women Practitioners of Medicine in the Middle Ages." *Proceedings of the Royal Society of Medicine* 15 (1922): 17–34.

Riddle, John M. *Contraception and Abortion from the Ancient World to the Renaissance.* Cambridge, Mass., 1992.

Robbins, Rossell Hope. "Medical Manuscripts in Middle English." *Speculum* 45 (1970): 393–415.

———. "Signs of Death in Middle English." *Medieval Studies* 32 (1970): 282–298.

Rotuli Hundredorum tempore Henry III, Edward I. London, 1818.

Rowland, Beryl. "Exhuming Trotula, Sapiens Matrona of Salerno." *Florilegium* 1(1979): 42–57.

———. *Medieval Woman's Guide to Health: The First English Gynecological Handbook.* Kent, 1981.

Sigerist, Henry. "The Regimen Sanitatis Salernitanum." *Landmarks in the History of Hygiene.* London, 1956.

Tacuinum Sanitatis. The Medieval Health Handbook. Luisa Cogliati Arano. Translated by Oscar Ratti and Adele Westbrook. New York, 1976.

Talbot, C. H. "Dame Trot and Her Progeny." *Essays and Studies* 25 (1972): 1–14.

———. *Medicine in Medieval England.* London, 1967.

Talbot, C. H., and E. A. Hammond. *The Medical Practitioners in Medieval England.* London, 1965.

Thorndike, Lynn. *History of Magic and Experimental Science.* New York, 1964.

———. "Hildegard of Bingen." In *History of Magic and Experimental Science.* Vol. 11. New York, 1964, pp. 124–54.

———. *University Records and Life in the Middle Ages.* New York, 1944.

Trotula of Salerno. *The Diseases of Women.* Translated by Elizabeth Mason-Hohl. Los Angeles, 1940.

Tuttle, Edward. "The Trotula and Old Dame Trot: A Note on the Lady of Salerno." *Bulletin of the History Medicine* 50 (1976): 61–72.

Wickersheimer, E., ed. *Commentaires de la faculté de médecine de l'Université de Paris 1395–1516.* Paris, 1950.

———. *Dictionnaire biographique des médecins en France au moyen ages.* Paris, 1936.

ON THE 14TH-CENTURY MASTER SURGEONS OATH:

This Latin document of the admission and oath of Master Surgeons of the City of London during the reign of King Richard II provides formulaic pledges for the Masters. Master surgeons were required to consult on difficult cases, to charge fair fees, to scrutinize the medical and surgical practices of both men and women practitioners, and to report any surgeons' errors and defaults to the mayor and aldermen. Promises in the document are so routine they are preceded with the word "etcetera," implying that any medieval reader should know what comes next.

Letter Book H, Folio 248 (1390).

ON MEDIEVAL MEDICAL MALPRACTICE LEGISLATION AND LITIGATION:

Cosman, Madeleine Pelner. "Dr. Elias Sabot and King Henry IV." *New York State Journal of Medicine* 69:18 (1969): 2482–90.

———. "Medieval Medical Malpractice and Chaucer's Physician." *New York State Journal of Medicine* 72:19 (1972): 2439–44.

————. "Medieval Medical Malpractice: the Dicta and Dockets." *Bulletin of the New York Academy of Medicine* 49 (1973): 22–47.

————. "Medical Fees, Fines, and Forfeits in Medieval England." *Man and Medicine* (1975): 133–58.

————. "Malpractice and Peer Review in Medieval England." *Transactions of the American Academy of Ophthalmology and Otolaryngology* 80 (May–June 1975): 293–297.

————. "Machaut's Medical Musical World." In *Machaut's World: Science and Art in the 14th Century,* edited by M. P. Cosman and Bruce Chandler, New York Academy of Sciences. New York, 1978.

————. "The Medieval Medical Third Party: Compulsory Consultation and Malpractice Insurance." *Annals of Plastic Surgery* 8, 2 (1982): 152–62.

————. "Pharmacology and the Pharmacopeia." In *Dictionary of the Middle Ages.* New York, 1982–7.

————. "A Feast for Aesculapius: Historical Diets for Asthma and Sexual Pleasure." *Annual Review of Nutrition* 3 (1983): 1–33.

————. "A Latin Medical Text Bibliography." A review of *Bibliographie des Textes Médicaux Latins: Antiquité et haut Moyen Age* by M. D. Grmek. *Journal of the History of Medicine and Allied Sciences* (April 1990).

————. "Past, Present, and Future in Medical Malpractice Litigation." *Journal of the History of Medicine and Allied Sciences* (June 1992).

————. "Surgical Malpractice in the Renaissance and Today." *Plastic and Reconstructive Surgery* (November, 1990).

————. "Surgical Malpractice in the Renaissance and Today." *Journal of the Florida Medical Association* (August 1991).

Cosman, Madeleine Pelner, and Sandra B. Katz. "Women in Medicine and Science." A review of L. Feibiger's *The Mind Has No Sex? Journal of the American Medical Association,* February 1987.

Cosman, Madeleine Pelner, and Ami Shah. "Medical Malpractice: Medieval and Modern." *National Trial Lawyer* 5:3 (September 1992).

ON DR. BARBARA OF WISSENKIRCHEN:
Friedenwald, Harry. "Jewish Doctoresses in the Middle Ages." In *The Jews and Medicine.* New York, 1967.

OBSTETRICS AND GYNECOLOGY
ON DR. TROTULA OF SALERNO:
Trotula of Salerno. *The Diseases of Women.* Translated by Elizabeth Mason-Hohl. Los Angeles, 1940.

————. *Medieval Woman's Guide to Health: The First English Gynecological Handbook.* Edited by Beryl Rowland. Kent, 1981.

NOTES AND REFERENCES
141

Aveling, J. H. "An Account of the Earliest English Work on Midwifery and the Diseases of Women." *Obstetrical Journal of Great Britain and Ireland* 14 (1874): 73–83.

Buhler, Curt F. "Prayers and Charms in Certain Middle English Scrolls." *Speculum* 39 (1964): 270–278.

Bullough, Vern. "Medieval Medical and Scientific Views of Women." In *Marriage in the Middle Ages,* edited by John Lyerle. *Viator* 4 (1973): 485–501.

————. *The Subordinate Sex: A History of Attitudes Towards Women.* Urbana, 1973.

Coleman, Emily. "Infanticide in the Early Middle Ages." In *Women in Medieval Society.* Edited by Susan M. Stuard. Philadelphia, 1976.

Cosman, Madeleine Pelner. "Criminalization of Abortion Knowledge." A review of John Riddle's *Eve's Herbs: A History of Contraception and Abortion in the West. Journal of the American Medical Association,* January 1998.

————. "Criminalization of Women and Trials of Witches." A review of Helen Rodnite Lemay's *Women's Secrets, Pseudo-Albertus Magnus' De Secretum Mulieris. Journal of the History of Medicine and Allied Sciences* (March 1994).

————. "Regulating Childbirth in Medical Law History." A review of John M. Riddle's *Contraception and Abortion from the Ancient World to the Renaissance. Journal of the American Medical Association,* May 1995.

De Renzi, S. *Collectio Salernitana.* Naples, 1852–1859.

Drabkin, Miriam, and Israel Drabkin. *Caelius Arelianus: Gynaecia.* Baltimore, 1941.

Forbes, T. R. *The Midwife and the Witch.* New Haven, 1966.

Gammer Gurton's Needle. Edited by J. S. Farmer. London, 1906.

Hamilton, George. "Trotula." *Modern Philology* 4 (1906): 377–380.

Himes, N. E. *A Medical History of Contraception.* Baltimore, 1936.

Hughes, M. *Women Healers in Medieval Life and Literature.* New York, 1943.

Kristeller, Paul Oskar. "The School of Salerno." *Bulletin of the History of Medicine* 17 (1945): 138–194.

Lawn, Brian. *The Salernitan Question.* Oxford, 1963.

Lemay, Helen Rodnite. *Women's Secrets, Pseudo-Albertus Magnus' De Secretum Mulieris.* Albany, 1992.

MacKinney, Loren. "Childbirth in the Middle Ages as Seen in Manuscripts." *Ciba Symposium* 8 (1960): 230–236.

Maubray, John. *The Female Physician.* London, 1724.

McLaren, Angus. *A History of Contraception from Antiquity to the Present Day.* London, 1990.

Mead, Kate Campbell-Hurd. *A History of Women in Medicine.* Haddam, 1938, Boston, 1973.

Miller, B. D. H. "She who hath drunk any potion." *Medium Aevum* 31 (1962): 188–193.

Noonan, J. T. *The Morality of Abortion: Legal and Historical Perspectives.* Cambridge, 1970.

———. *Contraception: A History of its Treatment by the Catholic Theologians and Canonists.* Cambridge, 1966.

Packard, F. R. *History of the School of Salernum.* New York, 1920.

Power, Eileen. "Some Women Practitioners of Medicine in the Middle Ages." *Proceedings of the Royal Society of Medicine* 15 (1922): 17–34.

Riddle, John. *Contraception and Abortion from the Ancient World to the Renaissance.* Cambridge, 1992.

———. *Eve's Herbs: A History of Contraception and Abortion in the West.* Cambridge, 1997.

Robbins, Rossell Hope. "Medical Manuscripts in Middle English." *Speculum* 45 (1970): 393–415.

Rowland, Beryl. "Exhuming Trotula, Sapiens Matrona of Salerno." *Florilegium* 1 (1979): 42–57.

———. *Chaucer and Middle English Studies in Honor of Rossell Hope Robbins.* London, 1974.

———. *Medieval Woman's Guide to Health: The First English Gynecological Handbook.* Kent, 1981.

Singer, Charles. *Studies in the History and Method of Science.* Oxford, 1917.

Singer, Charles, and Dorothea Singer. "The Origin of the Medical School of Salerno, the First University: An Attempted Reconstruction." In *Essays on the History of Medicine Presented to Karl Sudhoff.* London, 1924.

Talbot, C. H. "Dame Trot and Her Progeny." *Essays and Studies* 25 (1972): 1–14.

Thorndike, Lynn. *History of Magic and Experimental Science.* New York, 1964.

Tuttle, Edward. "The Trotula and Old Dame Trot: A Note on the Lady of Salerno." *Bulletin of the History of Medicine* 50 (1976): 61–72.

MEN AND WOMEN PATIENTS

ON DR. AGNES:
Rotuli Hundredorum tempore Henry III, Edward I. 2:646. London, 1818.
Talbot, C. H., and E. A. Hammond. *The Medical Practitioners in Medieval England.* London, 1965.

ON DR. JOHANNA:
Westminster Abbey Infirmarer's Rolls: 19400, 19401, 19402.
Power, Eileen, "Some Women Practitioners of Medicine in the Middle Ages." *Proceedings of the Royal Society of Medicine* 15 (1922): 17–34.
Talbot, C. H., and E. A. Hammond. *The Medical Practitioners in Medieval England.* London, 1965.

ON THE JEWISH WOMAN EYE SURGEON TREATING RABBI JUDAH:

Rabbi Judah ben Asher recorded his ocular tribulations and treatments in his testament.

Judah ben Asher. *The Testament of Rabbi Judah.* Edited by S. Schechter. Pressburg, 1885.

Friedenwald, Harry. "Jewish Doctoresses in the Middle Ages." In *The Jews and Medicine.* New York, 1967.

ON MEDIEVAL JEWISH WOMEN DOCTORS IN GERMANY:

Friedenwald, Harry. "Jewish Doctoresses in the Middle Ages." In *The Jews and Medicine.* New York, 1967.

Heffner, E. *Die Juden in Franken.* Stuttgart, 1855.

ON MEDICINAL APHRODISIACS:

Arano, Luisa Cogliati, ed. *The Medieval Health Handbook. Tacuinum Sanitatis.* Translated by Oscar Ratti and Adele Westbrook. New York, 1976.

Cosman, Madeleine Pelner. "Sex, Smut, Sin, and Spirit." In *Fabulous Feasts: Medieval Cookery and Ceremony.* New York, 1976, 1978, 1998.

———. "A Feast for Aesculapius: Historical Diets for Asthma and Sexual Pleasure. *Annals of Nutrition* 3 (1983): 1–33.

———. "The Taste of Medical Health." A review of L. G. Arano's *Medieval Health Handbook,* Tacuinum Sanitatis. The *Quarterly Review of Biology* (1977).

MEDICAL LICENSES
ON MEDIEVAL MEDICAL LICENSING:

Cosman, Madeleine Pelner. "Medieval Medical Malpractice and Chaucer's Physician." *New York State Journal of Medicine* 72:19 (1972): 2439–44.

———. "Medieval Medical Malpractice: the Dicta and Dockets." *Bulletin of the New York Academy of Medicine* 49:1 (1973): 22–47.

———. "Medical Fees, Fines, and Forfeits in Medieval England." *Man and Medicine* (1975): 133–58.

———. "Malpractice and Peer Review in Medieval England." *Transactions of the American Academy of Ophthalmology and Otolaryngology* 80 (May–June 1975): 293–297.

———. "Machaut's Medical Musical World." In *Machaut's World: Science and Art in the 14th Century,* edited by M. P. Cosman and Bruce Chandler, New York Academy of Sciences. New York, 1978.

Kibre, Pearl. "The Faculty of Medicine at Paris, Charlatanism, and Unlicensed Medical Practices in the Later Middle Ages." In *Legacies in Law and Medicine,* edited by C. R. Burns. New York, 1977.

MacKinney, Loren. "Medical Ethics and Etiquette in the Early Middle Ages: The Persistence of Hippocratic Ideals." In *Legacies in Law and Medicine,* edited by C. R. Burns. New York, 1977.

ON 14TH-CENTURY DR. VIRDIMURA OF CATANIA:

Friedenwald, Harry. "Jewish Doctoresses in the Middle Ages." In *The Jews and Medicine.* New York, 1967.
Revue des Etudes Juives 11: 287 (1900).

ON DR. SARAH OF WURTZBURG IN 1419:

Friedenwald, Harry. "Jewish Doctoresses in the Middle Ages." In *The Jews and Medicine.* New York, 1967.
Heffner, E. *Die Juden in Franken.* Stuttgart, 1855.

ON 14TH- AND 15TH-CENTURY PROSECUTIONS AGAINST UNLICENSED PRACTITIONERS IN FRANCE:

Kibre, Pearl. "The Faculty of Medicine at Paris, Charlatanism, and Unlicensed Medical Practices in the Later Middle Ages." In *Legacies in Law and Medicine,* edited by C. R. Burns. New York, 1977.
Wickersheimer, E., ed. *Commentaires de la faculté de médecine de l'Université de Paris 1395–1516.* Paris, 1950.
———. *Dictionnaire biographique des médecins en France au moyen ages.* Paris, 1936.

ON THE PREVALENCE OF WOMAN SURGEONS:

Perretta Petonne practiced surgery in her office on the Grande Rue St-Denis in Paris. During a long court battle beginning in 1410, she was prosecuted in January 1411 before Parliament by the Master Surgeons of Paris for practicing without a license. She asked in court for equal freedom from prosecution as other women surgeons in Paris enjoyed. However, an "examiner" forbade her to practice until she was examined and approved in conformity with city statutes and appropriately granted practice privileges. Dr. Perretta appeared before the masters and *jurati.* After the parties were heard, the case was continued to another day. But Petonne protested that she had office hours, "very sick patients" under her care who required her "essential medications and visitations." The court ordered her to deposit her surgery books with the provost for examination by four physicians of Paris plus the provost's criminal clerk, and she herself to be questioned by those physicians in the presence of two surgeons both parties trusted. The case was remitted for further adjudication in February. While the trial was pending, she was forbidden to practice and commanded to remove her surgeon's sign displayed on her office building.

Chartularium universitatis Parisiensis. Edited by H. Denifle and E. Chatelain (Paris, 1889–97): 198–199.

Thorndike, Lynn. *University Records and Life in the Middle Ages,* 289. New York, 1944.

ON THE PHARMACISTS' ORDINANCE OF 1322:

Chartularium universitatis Parisiensis. Edited by H. Denifle and E. Chatelain (Paris, 1889–97) 2: 268–269, no. 817; 2: 569, note 6.

MEDICAL MALPRACTICE CASES
ON DR. CLARICE DE ROTHOMAGO:

Her court case lasted for six months, from January 1312 through June 1312.

Chartularium universitatis Parisiensis. Edited by H. Denifle and E. Chatelain (Paris 1889–97) 2: 149–153.

Kibre, Pearl. "The Faculty of Medicine at Paris, Charlatanism, and Unlicensed Medical Practices in the Later Middle Ages." In *Legacies in Law and Medicine,* 58, edited by C. R. Burns. New York, 1977.

ON DR. JACQUELINE FELICIA DE ALMANIA:

Chartularium universitatis Parisiensis. Edited by H. Denifle and E. Chatelain (Paris 1889–97) 2: 255–266, no. 811.

Kibre, Pearl. "The Faculty of Medicine at Paris, Charlatanism, and Unlicensed Medical Practices in the Later Middle Ages." In *Legacies in Law and Medicine,* 59–63, edited by C. R. Burns. New York, 1977.

Wickersheimer, E. *Commentaires de la faculté de médecine de l'Université de Paris 1395–1516.* Paris, 1950.

ON DR. BRUNETTA OF TRENT:

Friedenwald, Harry. "Jewish Doctoresses in the Middle Ages." In *The Jews and Medicine.* New York, 1967.

Graetz, H. *Monatsschrift für die Geschichte und Wissenschaft des Judenthums.* Berlin, 1884.

———. *History of the Jews.* Philadelphia, 1891–1898.

LITERARY LADY DOCTORS
ON MARIE DE FRANCE'S LAIS:

Marie de France. *Lais.* Translated by Robert Hanning and Joan Ferrante. New York, 1978.

———. *Les lais.* Edited by Jean Rychner. Paris, 1966.

———. *Lais. Proud Knight, Fair Lady: The Twelve Lais of Marie de France.* Translated by Naomi Lewis. New York, 1989.

Burgess, Glyn S. *The Lais of Marie de France: Text and Context.* Athens, Georgia, 1987.

ON THE 13TH-CENTURY *SAINERESSE:*

Benson, Larry, and Theodore Andersson. *The Literary Context of Chaucer's Fabliaux.* Indianapolis and New York, 1971.

Montaiglon, L., and L. Raynaud. *Receuil general des fabliaux.* Paris, 1900.

MYSTERIOUS VANISHINGS OF MEDICAL WOMEN

ON DR. TROTULA OF SALERNO:

Trotula of Salerno. *The Diseases of Women.* Translated by Elizabeth Mason-Hohl. Los Angeles, 1940.

———. *Medieval Woman's Guide to Health: The First English Gynecological Handbook.* Edited by Beryl Rowland. Kent, 1981.

Aveling, J. H. "An Account of the Earliest English Work on Midwifery and the Diseases of Women." *Obstetrical Journal of Great Britain and Ireland* 14 (1874): 73–83.

Buhler, Curt F. "Prayers and Charms in Certain middle English Scrolls." *Speculum* 39 (1964): 270–278.

Bullough, Vern. "Medieval Medical and Scientific Views of Women." *Marriage in the Middle Ages.* Edited by John Lyerle. *Viator* 4 (1973): 485–501.

———. *The Subordinate Sex: A History of Attitudes Towards Women.* Urbana, 1973.

Coleman, Emily. "Infanticide in the Early Middle Ages." In *Women in Medieval Society,* edited by Susan M. Stuard. Philadelphia, 1976.

Cosman, Madeleine Pelner. "Criminalization of Abortion Knowledge." A review of John Riddle's Eve's Herbs: A History of Contraception and Abortion in the West. *Journal of the American Medical Association* (January 1998).

———. "Criminalization of Women and Trials of Witches." A review of Helen Rodnite Lemay's *Women's Secrets, Pseudo-Albertus Magnus' De Secretum Mulieris. Journal of the History of Medicine and Allied Sciences* (March 1994).

———. "Regulating Childbirth in Medical Law History." A review of John M. Riddle's *Contraception and Abortion from the Ancient World to the Renaissance. Journal of the American Medical Association,* May 1995.

De Renzi, S. *Collectio Salernitana.* Naples, 1852–1859.

Drabkin, Miriam, and Israel Drabkin, eds. *Caelius Arelianus: Gynaecia.* Baltimore, 1941.

Forbes, T. R. *The Midwife and the Witch.* New Haven, 1966.

Gammer Gurton's Needle. Edited by J. S. Farmer. London, 1906.

Hamilton, George. "Trotula." *Modern Philology* 4 (1906): 377–380.

Himes, N. E. *A Medical History of Contraception.* Baltimore, 1936.

Hughes, M. *Women Healers in Medieval Life and Literature.* New York, 1943.

Kristeller, Paul Oskar. "The School of Salerno." *Bulletin of the History of Medicine* 17 (1945): 138–194.

Lawn, Brian. *The Salernitan Question.* Oxford, 1963.

Lemay, Helen Rodnite. *Women's Secrets, Pseudo-Albertus Magnus' De Secretum Mulieris.* Albany, 1992.

MacKinney, Loren. "Childbirth in the Middle Ages as Seen in Manuscripts." *Ciba Symposium* 8 (1960): 230–236.

Maubray, John. *The Female Physician.* London, 1724.

McLaren, Angus. *A History of Contraception from Antiquity to the Present Day.* London, 1990.

Mead, Kate Campbell-Hurd. *A History of Women in Medicine.* Haddam, 1938, Boston, 1973.

Miller, B. D. H. "She who hath drunk any potion." *Medium Aevum* 31 (1962): 188–193.

Noonan, J. T. *The Morality of Abortion: Legal and Historical Perspectives.* Cambridge, 1970.

———. *Contraception: A History of its Treatment by the Catholic Theologians and Canonists.* Cambridge, 1966.

Packard, F. R. *History of the School of Salernum.* New York, 1920.

Power, Eileen, "Some Women Practitioners of Medicine in the Middle Ages." *Proceedings of the Royal Society of Medicine* 15 (1922): 17–34.

Riddle, John. *Contraception and Abortion from the Ancient World to the Renaissance.* Cambridge, 1992.

———. *Eve's Herbs: A History of Contraception and Abortion in the West.* Cambridge, 1997.

Robbins, Rossell Hope. "Medical Manuscripts in Middle English." *Speculum* 45 (1970): 393–415.

Rowland, Beryl. "Exhuming Trotula, Sapiens Matrona of Salerno." *Florilegium* 1 (1979): 42–57.

———. *Chaucer and Middle English Studies in Honor of Rossell Hope Robbins.* London, 1974.

———. *Medieval Woman's Guide to Health: The First English Gynecological Handbook.* Kent, 1981.

Singer, Charles. *Studies in the History and Method of Science.* Oxford, 1917.

Singer, Charles, and Dorothea Singer. "The Origin of the Medical School of Salerno, the First University: An Attempted Reconstruction." *Essays on the History of Medicine presented to Karl Sudhoff.* London, 1924.

Talbot, C. H. "Dame Trot and Her Progeny." *Essays and Studies* 25 (1972): 1–14.

Thorndike, Lynn. *History of Magic and Experimental Science.* New York, 1964.

Tuttle, Edward. "The Trotula and Old Dame Trot: A Note on the Lady of Salerno." *Bulletin of the History of Medicine* 50 (1976): 61–72.

ON DR. HILDEGARD OF BINGEN:

Hildegard of Bingen. "Liber Subtilitatum." In *Patrologia Latina.* Vol. 197. Edited by J. P. Migne. Paris, 1882.

———. "Vita Sanctae Hildegardis." In *Patrologia Latina.* Vol. 197. Edited by J. P. Migne. Paris, 1882.

———. *Causae et Curae.* Edited by Paul Kaiser. Leipzig, 1903.

Engbring, G. M. "Saint Hildegard, Twelfth Century Physician." *Bulletin of the History of Medicine* 8 (1940): 770–784.

Hopkins, Andrea. *Most Wise and Valiant Ladies. Remarkable Lives of Women in the Middle Ages.* London, 1997.

Singer, Charles. *Studies in the History and Method of Science.* Oxford, 1917.

Singer, Charles, and Dorothea Singer. "The Origin of the Medical School of Salerno, the First University: An Attempted Reconstruction." *Essays on the History of Medicine presented to Karl Sudhoff.* London, 1924.

Thorndike, Lynn. "Hildegard of Bingen." *History of Magic and Experimental Science* vol. 11, 124–54. New York, 1964.

———. *History of Magic and Experimental Science.* New York, 1964.

Chapter 3

LADY BOSSES: RULERS OF MANORS AND MONASTERIES

ON MEDIEVAL WOMEN IN POWER:

Aquinas, St. Thomas. *Summa Theologica.* Translated by the Fathers of the English Dominican Province. London, 1912.

Arthur, Marylin B. "Early Greece: The Origins of the Western Attitude Toward Women." *Arethusa* 6 (Spring, 1973).

Asociación Cultural Al-Mudayna. *Las Sabias mujeres: educación, saber y autoraia siglos III–XVII.* Madrid, 1994.

Augustine, Saint. *The City of God.* Translated by Henry Bettonson. Harmondsworth, 1972.

Baker, Derek. *Medieval Women.* Oxford, 1978.

Barber, Elizabeth. *Women's Work: the First 20,000 Years.* New York, 1994.

Barratt, Alexandra. *Women's Writing in Middle English.* London, New York, 1992.

Barth, Susanne. *Jungfrauenzucht: literaturwissenschaftliche und pedagogische Studien zur Meadchenerziehungsliteratur zwischen 1200 und 1600.* Stuttgart, 1994.

Bateson, Mary. "Origin and Early History of Double Monasteries," In *Transactions of the Royal Historical Society* n.s.13 (1899): 137–198.

Bennet, H. S. *The Pastons and Their England.* Cambridge, 1951.

Bitel, Lisa. *Land of Women: Tales of Sex and Gender from Early Ireland.* Ithaca and London, 1996.

Bolton, Brenda. "Mulieres Sanctae." In *Women in Medieval Society,* edited by Susan Stuard. Philadelphia, 1976.

Bornstein, Diane. "The Ideal of the Lady of the Manor as Reflected in Christine de Pizan's *Livre des Trois Vertus.*" In *Ideals for Women in the Works of Christine de Pizan,* edited by Diane Bornstein, 117–128. Michigan, 1981.

————. *Mirrors of Courtesy.* Hamden, Conn., 1965.

Borreson, Kari Elizabeth. *Subordination and Equivalence: The Nature and Role of Women in Augustine and Thomas Aquinas.* Washington, 1981.

Brown, S., and J. O'Sullivan. *The Register of Eudes of Rouen.* New York, 1964.

Butler, Melissa. "Early Liberal Roots of Feminism: John Locke and the Attack on Patriarchy." *American Political Science Review* 72 (March 1978): 135–50.

Bynum, Caroline Walker. *Holy Feast and Holy Fast.* Berkeley, 1987.

————. *Jesus as Mother: Studies in the Spirituality of the High Middle Ages.* Berkeley, 1982.

Cartellieri, Otto. *The Court of Burgundy.* New York, 1970.

Cherewatuk, Karen and Ulrike Wiethaus. *Dear Sister: Medieval Women and the Epistolary Genre.* Philadelphia, 1993.

Christine de Pizan. *The Book of the Three Virtues.* Translated by Charity Cannon Willard and Madeleine Pelner Cosman as *Medieval Women's Mirror of Honor: The Treasury of the City of Ladies.* New York, 1989.

Cosman, Madeleine Pelner. *The Education of the Hero in Arthurian Romance.* Chapel Hill, 1966.

————. *Fabulous Feasts: Medieval Cookery and Ceremony.* New York, 1976, 1978, 1998.

————. "Christine de Pizan's Well-Tempered Feminism." *Helicon Nine, a Journal of Women's Arts and Letters.* 1984.

Davis, Natalie Zemon. *Society and Culture in Early Modern France.* Stanford, 1965.

Dillard, Heath. "Women in Reconquest Castille." In *Women in Medieval Society,* edited by S. Stuard. Philadelphia, 1976.

————. *Daughters of the Reconquest: Women in Castillian Town Society.* New York, 1984.

Drew, Katherine Fisher. *The Lombard Laws.* Philadelphia, 1973.

Dronke, Peter. *Abelard and Heloise in Medieval Testimonies.* Totowa, N.J., 1977.

Duby, Georges. *The Knight, the Lady and the Priest: The Making of Modern Marriage in Medieval France.* Translated by Barbara Bray. New York, 1984.

Duckett, Eleanor Shipley. *Women and their Letters in the Early Middle Ages.* Northampton, 1964.

Dufournet, Jean, Pierre Toubert, Rita Lejeune, et al. *Femmes, Mariage-Lignages xii–xiv siècles: Melanges offerts à Georges Duby.* Brussels, 1992.

Dulac, Liliane, "Inspiration mystique et savoir politique: les conseils aux veuves chez Francesco da Barbarino et chez Christine de Pizan." In *Melanges a la Memoire de Franco Simone*, 113–141. Geneva, 1990.

Elkenstein, Lina. *Women Under Monasticism*. Cambridge, 1896, 1922.

Elshtain, Jean Bethke. *Public Man, Private Woman: Women in Social and Political Thought*. Princeton, 1981.

———. "Moral Woman and Immoral Man: A Consideration of the Public-Private Split and Its Political Ramifications." *Politics and Society* 4 (1974): 453–73.

Erler, Mary, and Maryanne Kowalski, eds. *Women and Power in the Middle Ages*. Athens, Georgia, 1988.

Evergates, Theodore. *Aristocratic Women in Medieval France*. Philadelphia, 1999.

Facinger, Marion. "A Study of Medieval Queenship: Capetian France 987–1237," In *Studies in Medieval and Renaissance History*, edited by William Bowsky. Lincoln, 1968.

Ferrante, Joan M. *To the Glory of Her Sex: Women's Roles in the Composition of Medieval Texts*. Bloomington, 1997.

Figueiredo, A. J. de. "Espelho de Cristina." *Revista Brasileira de Folologia* 3 (1957): 117–119.

Filmer, Robert, Sir. "Patriarcha." Refuted in John Locke's *Two Treatises of Government*, edited by T. I. Cook. New York, 1947.

Fraser, Antonia. *Warrior Queens*. New York, 1990.

Fustel de Coulanges, Numa Denis. *The Ancient City*. Baltimore and London, 1980.

Gies, Frances and Joseph Gies. *Marriage and the Family in the Middle Ages*. New York, 1987.

———. *Women in the Middle Ages*. New York, 1978.

Glente, Karen, and Lise Winther-Jensen. *Female Power in the Middle Ages*. Copenhagen, 1989.

Godfrey, J. "The Double Monastery in Early English History," *AJ* 79 (1974): 19–32.

Gold, Penny Schine. *The Lady and the Virgin: Image, Attitude, and Experience in 12th-century France*. Chicago, 1987.

Goldberg, P. J. P. *Woman Is a Worthy Wight: Women in English Society 1200–1500*. Phoenix Mill, U.K., and Wolfeboro Falls, N.H., 1992.

Goldthwaite, Richard. "The Florentine Palace as Domestic Architecture." *American Historical Review* 72 (1972): 1011.

Gulati, Saroj. *Women and Society: Northern India in 11th and 12th Century*. Delhi, 1985.

Harksen, Sibylle. *Women in the Middle Ages*. New York, 1975.

Harrad of Landsberg. *Hortus Deliciarum*. Facsimile edition by Caratzas Brothers. New York, 1977.

Harrison, A. W. R. *The Law of Athens: The Family and Property*. Oxford, 1968.

Harvey, Ruth. *Marquard vom Stein, der Ritter vom Turn*. Berlin, 1996.

Heinrich, Mary Pia. *The Canonesses and Education in the Early Middle Ages*. Washington, 1924.

Hentsch, Alice A. *De la littérature didactique du moyen age s'adressant spécialement aux femmes.* Geneva, 1975.

Herlihy, David. *Medieval Households.* Cambridge, 1985.

————. "Land, Family, and Women in Continental Europe." In *Women in Medieval Society,* edited by S. Stuard. Philadelphia, 1976.

————. *Opera Muliebra: Women and Work in Medieval Europe.* New York, 1990.

Hindman, Sandra L. *Christine de Pizan's "Epistre d'Othea," Painting and Politics at the Court of Charles VI.* Toronto, 1988.

Hobbes, Thomas. *Leviathan.* Edited by C. B. Macpherson. Harmondsworth, 1968.

Holloway, Julia B; Constance S. Wright; and Joan Bechtold. *Equally in God's Image: Women in the Middle Ages.* New York, 1990.

Jacobius, Helene. *Die erziehung des edelfreauleins im alten Frankreich nach dichtungen des XII., XIII. and XIV. jahrhunderts.* Halle, 1908.

Jaeger, Werner. *Five Essays.* Translated by Adele M. Fiske. Montreal, 1966.

Kelly, Amy. *Eleanore of Aquitaine and the Four Kings.* Cambridge, 1952.

King, Margaret L., and Albert Rabil, Jr. *Her Immaculate Hand: Selected Works by and about the Women Humanists of Quattrocento Italy.* Binghamton, 1992, 1997.

Krauss, Henry. *The Living Theater of Medieval Art.* Philadelphia, 1967.

Labarge, Margaret Wade. *Women in Medieval Life: A Small Sound of the Trumpet.* London, 1986.

Laigle, Mathilde. *Le Livre des Trois Vertus de Christine de Pisan et son milieu historique et littéraire.* Paris, 1912.

La Tour Landry, Geoffrey de. *The Book of the Knight of La Tour-Landry Compiled for the Instruction of His Daughters.* Translated by Thomas Wright. London, 1906.

Leibell, Jane Frances, Sister. *Anglo-Saxon Education of Women: from Hilda to Hildegarde.* New York, 1971.

Lenzi, Maria Ludovica. *Donne e madonne: l'educazione femminile nel primo Rinascimento italiano.* Turin, 1982.

Leon, Vicki. *Uppity Women of Medieval Times.* Berkeley, 1997.

Lewis, Gertrud Jargon. *By Women, for Women, about Women: The Sister-Books of Fourteenth-Century Germany.* Toronto, 1996.

Locke, John. *Two Treatises of Civil Government.* Edited by Thomas Cook. New York, 1947.

Lucas, Angela. *Women in the Middle Ages: Religion, Marriage, and Letters.* New York, 1983.

Mate, Mavis E. *Daughters, Wives, and Widows After the Black Death: Women in Sussex 1350–1525.* Woodbridge, U.K., and Rochester, N.Y., 1998.

McLaughlin, Eleanor Commo. "Women, Power, and the Pursuit of Holiness in Medieval Christianity." In *Women of Spirit: Female Leadership in the Jewish and Christian Tradition,* edited by Rosemary Radford Ruether and Eleanor McLaughlin. New York, 1979.

————. "Equality of Souls, Inequality of Sexes: Woman in Medieval Theology." In *Religion and Sexism: Images of Woman in the Jewish and Christian Traditions,* edited by Rosemary Radford Ruether. New York, 1974.

McNamara, Jo Ann. "Sexual Equality and the Cult of Virginity in Early Christian Thought." *Feminist Studies* 3, 4 (Spring-Summer 1976): 144–58.

McNamara, Jo Ann, and Suzanne F. Wemple. "Sanctity and Power: The Dual Pursuit of Medieval Women." In *Becoming Visible: Women in European History,* edited by Renate Bridenthal and Claudia Koonz. Boston, 1974.

Meade, M. *Eleanore of Aquitaine.* New York, 1977.

Meale, Carol. *Women and Literature in Britain, 1150–1500.* Cambridge, New York, 1993.

Meek, Christine and Katherine Simms. *'The Fragility of Her Sex'? Medieval Irishwomen in Their European Context.* Dublin, 1996.

Morris, Joan. *The Lady Was a Bishop.* New York, 1973.

Nelson, Janet. "Queens as Jezebels: The Careers of Brunhild and Balthild in Merovingian History." In *Medieval Women,* edited by Derek Baker. Oxford, 1978.

Netanyahu, B. *The Marranos of Spain from the Late XIVth to the Early XVIth Century.* New York, 1966.

Nolan, Edward Peter. *Cry Out and Write: A Feminine Poetics of Revelation.* New York, 1994.

Okin, Susan Moller. *Women in Western Political Thought.* Princeton, 1979.

Painter, Sidney. *French Chivalry.* Baltimore, 1940.

Parducci, Amos. *Costumi ornati; studi sugli insegnamenti di cortigiania medievali.* Bologna, 1928.

Parvey, Constance F. "The Theology and Leadership of Women in the New Testament." In *Religion and Sexism: Images of Woman in the Jewish and Christian Traditions,* edited by Rosemary Radford Ruether. New York, 1974.

Paston Letters. Edited by James Gairdner. London, 1896.

Paston Letters. Edited by N. Davis. London, 1958.

Phillpotts, Bertha. *Kindred and Clan in the Middle Ages and After.* Cambridge, 1913.

Pitkin, Hanna F. *Fortune Is a Woman: Gender and Politics.* Berkeley, 1984.

Plumpton Correspondence. Edited by T. Stapleton. London, 1839.

Pomeroy, Sarah B. *Goddesses, Whores, Wives and Slaves.* New York, 1975.

Postan, M. M. *Medieval Women.* Cambridge, 1975.

Potkay, Monica Brzezinski and Regula Meyer Evitt. *Minding the Body: Women and Literature in the Middle Ages, 800–1500.* London, New York, 1997.

Power, Eileen, ed. *The Goodman of Paris.* London, 1928.

————. *Medieval English Nunneries.* Cambridge, 1922.

Richards, Earl Jeffrey. "Christine de Pizan and the Question of Feminist Rhetoric." In *Modern Language Association Conference* 22: 15–24 (1983).

Rogers, Katherine M. *The Troublesome Helpmate: A History of Misogyny in Literature.* Seattle, 1966.

Ruddick, Sara. "Maternal Thinking." *Feminist Studies* 6 (1980): 343–67.

Ruether, Rosemary. "Mothers of the Church: Ascetic Women in the Late Patristic Age." In *Women of Spirit: Female Leadership in the Jewish and Christian Traditions,* edited by Rosemary Ruether and Eleanor McLaughlin. New York, 1970.

———. "Virginal Feminism in the Fathers of the Church." In *Religion and Sexism: Images of Woman in the Jewish and Christian Traditions,* edited by Rosemary Radford Ruether. New York, 1974.

Ruhmer, Wilhelm. *Peadagogische theorien euber frauenbildung im zeitalter der renaissance.* Bonn, 1915.

Russell, Josiah Cox. *Late Ancient and Medieval Population.* Philadelphia, 1958.

Russell, Rinaldin. *Italian Women Writers: A Bio-Bibliographical Sourcebook.* Westport, 1994.

Saxonhouse, Arlene W. *Women in the History of Political Thought.* New York, 1985.

Schochet, Gordon J. *Patriarchalism in Political Thought.* New York, 1975.

Schussler-Fiorenza, Elisabeth. *In Memory of Her: A Feminist Theological Reconstruction of Christian Origins.* New York, 1983.

Sherman, C. R. "The Queen in Charles V's Coronation Book." In *Viator* (Berkeley 1977): 255.

Smith, Jacqueline. "Robert of Arbrissel: Procurator Mulierum." In *Medieval Women,* edited by Derek Baker. Oxford, 1978.

Spelman, Elizabeth V. "Woman as Body: Ancient and Contemporary Views." *Feminist Studies* 8 (Spring 1982): 109–30.

Stafford, Pauline. *Queens, Concubines, and Dowagers: The King's Wife in the Early Middle Ages.* New York, 1983.

———. *Queen Emma and Queen Edith: Queenship and Women's Power in Eleventh Century England.* Malden, Massachusetts, 1997.

Stenton, Doris. *The English Woman in History.* London and New York, 1957.

Stolingwa, Peter. *Zum livre du chevalier de La Tour Landry pour l'enseignement de ses filles.* Breslau, 1906.

Stuard, Susan Mosher. *Women in Medieval History and Historiography.* Philadelphia, 1987.

Vincent of Beauvais. *De eruditione filiorum nobilium.* Translated by Rosemary Barton Tobin. New York, 1984.

———. *De eruditione filiorum nobilium.* Edited by Arpad Steiner. Cambridge, 1938, New York, 1970.

———. *On the Education of Noble Children.* Translated by William Ellwood Craig. New York, 1949.

Walker, S. S. "Widow and Ward: The Feudal Law of Child Custody." In *Women in Medieval Society,* edited by S. Stuard. Philadelphia, 1976.

Ward, Jennifer. *Women of the English Nobility and Gentry 1066–1500.* New York, 1995.

Wemple, Suzanne Fonay. *Women in Frankish Society: Marriage and the Cloister 500 to 900.* Philadelphia, 1981.

Wheeler, Bonnie. *Representations of the Feminine in the Middle Ages.* Dallas, 1993.

Willard, Charity Cannon. "A Portuguese Translation of Christine de Pizan's Livre des Trois Vertus." *PMLA* 78 (1963): 459–464.

Wolff, Hans Julius. "Marriage Law and Family Organization in Ancient Athens: A Study of the Interrelation of Public and Private Law in the Greek City." *Traditio* 2 (1944): 43–95.

Wrigley, E. A. *Population and History.* New York, 1969.

ON QUEEN ELEANOR OF AQUITAINE:

Kelly, Amy. *Eleanore of Aquitaine and the Four Kings.* Cambridge, 1952.

Meade, M. *Eleanore of Aquitaine.* New York, 1977.

DIRECTING THE HOUSEHOLD

ON THE EDUCATION OF MEDIEVAL WOMEN:

Asociación Cultural Al-Mudayna. *Las Sabias mujeres: educación, saber y autoraia siglos III–XVII.* Madrid, 1994.

Barth, Susanne. *Jungfrauenzucht: Literaturwissenschaftliche und peadagogische Studien zur Meadchenerziehungsliteratur zwischen 1200 und 1600.* Stuttgart, 1994.

Cherewatuk, Karen and Ulrike Wiethaus. *Dear Sister: Medieval Women and the Epistolary Genre.* Philadelphia, 1993.

Eckenstein, Lina. *Women Under Monasticism.* Cambridge, 1896, 1922.

Ferrante, Joan M. *To the Glory of Her Sex: Women's Roles in the Composition of Medieval Texts.* Bloomington, 1997.

Heinrich, Mary Pia. *The Canonesses and Education in the Early Middle Ages.* Washington, 1924.

Hentsch, Alice A. *De la littérature didactique du moyen age s'adressant spécialement aux femmes.* Geneva, 1975.

Jacobius, Helene. *Die erziehung des edelfrauleins im alten Frankreich nach dichtungen des XII., XIII. und XIV. jahrhunderts.* Halle, 1908.

King, Margaret L., and Albert Rabil, Jr. *Her Immaculate Hand: Selected Works by and about the Women Humanists of Quattrocento Italy.* Binghamton, 1992, 1997.

La Tour Landry, Geoffrey de. *The Book of the Knight of La Tour-Landry Compiled for the Instruction of his Daughters.* Translated by Thomas Wright. London, 1906.

Leibell, Jane Frances, Sister. *Anglo-Saxon Education of Women: from Hilda to Hildegarde.* New York, 1971.

Lenzi, Maria Ludovica. *Donne e madonne: l'educazione femminile nel primo Rinascimento italiano.* Turin, 1982.

Lewis, Katherine; Noel Menuge; and Kim Phillips. *Young Medieval Women.* Stroud, 1999.

Ruhmer, Wilhelm. *Peadagogische theorien euber frauenbildung im zeitalter der renaissance.* Bonn, 1915.

Russell, Rinaldin. *Italian Women Writers: A Bio-Bibliographical Sourcebook.* Westport, 1994.

Stolingwa, Peter. *Zum livre du chevalier de La Tour Landry pour l'enseignement de ses filles.* Breslau, 1906.

Vincent of Beauvais. *De eruditione filiorum nobilium.* Edited by Arpad Steiner. Cambridge, 1938; New York, 1970.

————. *De eruditione filiorum nobilium.* Translated by Rosemary Barton Tobin. New York, 1984.

————. *On the Education of Noble Children.* Translated by William Ellwood Craig. New York, 1949.

ON WOMEN PATRONS OF THE ARTS:

Barratt, Alexandra. *Women's Writing in Middle English.* London, New York, 1992.

Bornstein, Diane. *Mirrors of Courtesy.* Hamden, Conn, 1975.

Cherewatuk, Karen and Ulrike Wiethaus. *Dear Sister: Medieval Women and the Epistolary Genre.* Philadelphia, 1993.

Duckett, Eleanor. *Women and Their Letters in the Early Middle Ages.* Northampton, 1964.

Ferrante, Joan M. *To the Glory of Her Sex: Women's Roles in the Composition of Medieval Texts.* Bloomington, 1997.

————. *Woman as Image in Medieval Literature.* New York, 1976.

Ferrier, Janet. *Forerunners of the French Novel: An Essay on the Development of the Novella in the Late Middle Ages.* London, 1954.

Hentsch, Alice A. *De la littérature didactique du moyen age s'adressant spécialement aux femmes.* Geneva, 1975.

Holloway, Julia B; Constance S. Wright; and Joan Bechtold. *Equally in God's Image: Women in the Middle Ages.* New York, 1990.

Kemp-Welch, Alice. *Of Six Medieval Women.* London, 1913.

King, Margaret L. and Albert Rabil, Jr. *Her Immaculate Hand: Selected Works by and about the Women Humanists of Quattrocento Italy.* Binghamton, 1992, 1997.

Lucas, Angela. *Women in the Middle Ages: Religion, Marriage, and Letters.* New York, 1983.

Meale, Carol. *Women and Literature in Britain, 1150–1500.* Cambridge, New York, 1993.

Meiss, Millard. *French Painting in the Time of Jean, Duc de Berry.* London, 1967.

Morewedge, Rosemarie Thee, ed. *The Role of Woman in the Middle Ages.* Albany, 1975.

Pernoud, Regine. *Blanche of Castille.* New York, 1975.

Russell, Rinaldin. *Italian Women Writers: a Bio-Bibliographical Sourcebook.* Westport, 1994.

Solente, S., ed. *Le Livre de la Mutation de Fortune, par Christine de Pisan.* Paris, 1959–1968.

Vetere, Benedetto, and Paolo Renzi, eds. *Profili di donne.* Galatina, 1986.

Willard, Charity Cannon. *Development of the Novella in the Late Middle Ages.* London, 1954.

———. "A Fifteenth-Century View of Women's Role in Medieval Society." In *The Role of Woman in the Middle Ages,* edited by Rosemarie Morewedge. Albany, 1975.

———. *The Livre de la Paix of Christine de Pisan.* 'S Gravenhage, 1958.

Willard, Charity Cannon and Madeleine Pelner Cosman. *Medieval Woman's Mirror of Honor: The Treasury of the City of Ladies,* a translation of *The Book of Three Virtues* by Christine de Pizan. New York, 1989.

ON MARGARET PASTON:

The Paston Letters. Edited by James Gairdner. London, 1896.

The Paston Letters. Edited by N. Davis. London, 1958.

Bennet, H. S. *The Pastons and Their England.* Cambridge, 1951.

Duckett, Eleanor Shipley. *Women and their Letters in the Early Middle Ages.* Northampton, 1964.

Hopkins, Andrea. *Most Wise and Valiant Ladies: Remarkable Lives of Women in the Middle Ages.* London, 1997.

Power, Eileen. *Medieval Women.* Edited by M. M. Postan. Cambridge, 1976.

ON CHRISTINE DE PIZAN'S *BOOK OF THREE VIRTUES* ALSO CALLED *THE TREASURY OF THE CITY OF LADIES:*

Christine de Pizan. *The Book of the Three Virtues.* Translated by Charity Cannon Willard and Madeleine Pelner Cosman. *Medieval Women's Mirror of Honor: The Treasury of the City of Ladies.* New York, 1989.

Bornstein, Diane. "The Ideal of the Lady of the Manor as Reflected in Christine de Pizan's *Livre des Trois Vertus.*" In *Ideals for Women in the Works of Christine de Pizan,* edited by Diane Bornstein, 117–128. Michigan, 1981.

———. *Mirrors of Courtesy.* Hamden, Conn., 1965.

Cosman, Madeleine Pelner. "Christine de Pizan's Well-Tempered Feminism." *Helicon Nine, a Journal of Women's Arts and Letters.* 1984.

Dulac, Liliane, "Inspiration mystique et savoir politique: les conseils aux veuves chez Francesco da Barbarino et chez Christine de Pizan." In *Melanges a la Mémoire de Franco Simone* 113–141. Geneva, 1980.

Laigle, Mathilde. *Le Livre des Trois Vertus de Christine de Pisan et son milieu historique et littéraire.* Paris, 1912.

Willard, Charity Cannon. "A Portuguese Translation of Christine de Pizan's *Livre des Trois Vertus.*" *PMLA* 78 (1963): 459–464.

ON THE GOODMAN OF PARIS:

Power, Eileen, ed. *The Goodman of Paris,* London, 1928.

ON STALWART SCOTTISH WOMEN DEFENDING THEIR CASTLES:

Burton, J. H. *History of Scotland,* 3: 21. London, 1867.

Turnbull, W. B., ed. *The Buik of the Croniclis of Scotland* 3: 341–342. London, 1858.

ON ALICE KNYVET'S BATTLE:

During the reign of King Edward IV, she held her Bokenham Castle, helped by 50 people wielding swords, glaives, and bows and arrows.

Public Record Office, London. *Calendar of the Patent Rolls 1461–1467.* London, 1907.

ARRANGED MARRIAGE

ON MEDIEVAL MARRIAGE:

Bynum, Caroline Walker. *Holy Feast and Holy Fast: The Religious Significance of Food to Medieval Women.* Berkeley, 1987.

Duby, Georges. *The Knight, the Lady and the Priest: The Making of Modern Marriage in Medieval France.* Translated by Barbara Bray. New York, 1984.

Dufournet, Jean; Pierre Toubert; Rita Lejeune; et al. *Femmes, Mariage-Lignages xii–xiv siècles: Melanges offerts à Georges Duby.* Brussels, 1992.

Falk, Ze'ev W. *Jewish Matrimonial Law in the Middle Ages.* Oxford, 1966.

Gies, Frances and Joseph Gies. *Marriage and the Family in the Middle Ages.* New York, 1987.

Gold, Penny Schine. *The Lady and the Virgin: Image, Attitude, and Experience in 12th-Century France.* Chicago, 1987.

Goody, Jack. *The Development of the Family and Marriage in Europe.* New York, 1983.

Herlihy, David. *Medieval Households.* Cambridge, 1985.

———. "Life Expectancies of Medieval Women." In *The Role of Women in the Middle Ages,* edited by Rosmarie Morewedge. Albany, 1975.

———. "Land, Family, and Women in Continental Europe." In *Women in Medieval Society,* edited by Susan Mosher Stuard. Philadelphia, 1976.

———. *Opera Muliebra: Women and Work in Medieval Europe.* New York, 1990.

Holloway, Julia B; Constance S. Wright; and Joan Bechtold. *Equally in God's Image: Women in the Middle Ages.* New York, 1990.

Klapisch-Zuber, Christiane. "Women and the Family." In *Medieval Callings,* edited by Jacques Le Goff. Chicago, 1990.

Laslett, P. and R. Wald. *Household and Family in Past Time.* Cambridge, 1972.

Lyerle, John, ed. *Marriage in the Middle Ages, Viator* 4 (1973).

Mate, Mavis E. *Daughters, Wives, and Widows After the Black Death: Women in Sussex 1350–1525.* Woodbridge, U.K., and Rochester, N.Y., 1998.

McNamara, Jo Ann. "Sexual Equality and the Cult of Virginity in Early Christian Thought." *Feminist Studies* 3, 4 (Spring-Summer 1976): 144–58.

McNamara, Jo Ann, and Suzanne F. Wemple. "Sanctity and Power: The Dual Pursuit of Medieval Women." In *Becoming Visible: Women in European History,* edited by Renate Bridenthal and Claudia Koonz. Boston, 1974.

Nelson, Janet. "Queens as Jezebels: The Careers of Brunhild and Balthild in Merovingian History." In *Medieval Women,* edited by Derek Baker. Oxford, 1978.

Nicholas, David. *The Domestic Life of a Medieval City: Women, Children and the Family in 14th-Century Ghent.* Lincoln, 1985.

Parvey, Constance F. "The Theology and Leadership of Women in the New Testament." In *Religion and Sexism: Images of Woman in the Jewish and Christian Traditions,* edited by Rosemary Radford Ruether. New York, 1974.

Pomeroy, Sarah B. *Goddesses, Whores, Wives and Slaves.* New York, 1975.

Stafford, Pauline. *Queens, Concubines, and Dowagers: The King's Wife in the Early Middle Ages.* New York, 1983.

Stuard, Susan Mosher. *Women in Medieval History and Historiography.* Philadelphia, 1987.

Walker, S. S. "Widow and Ward: The Feudal Law of Child Custody." In *Women in Medieval Society,* edited by S. Stuard. Philadelphia, 1976.

Wemple, Suzanne Fonay. *Women in Frankish Society: Marriage and the Cloister 500 to 900.* Philadelphia, 1981.

Wolff, Hans Julius. "Marriage Law and Family Organization in Ancient Athens: A Study of the Interrelation of Public and Private Law in the Greek City." *Traditio* 2 (1944): 43–95.

ON EUGINIA PICOT AND WIDOWHOOD:

Bird, W. H. B., ed. *Calendar of the Close Rolls.* London, 1927.

Bennett, Judith. *A Medieval Life: Cecilia Penifader of Brigstock, 1295–1344.* Boston, 1999.

Christine de Pizan. *The Book of the Three Virtues.* Translated by Charity Cannon Willard and Madeleine Pelner Cosman. Published as *A Medieval Woman's Mirror of Honor.* New York, 1989.

Duby, Georges. *Women of the Twelfth Century: Remembering the Dead.* Chicago, 1997.

Greilsammer, Myriam. *L'envers du Tableau: Mariage et Maternité en Flandre médiévale.* Paris, 1990.

Heene, Katrien. *The Legacy of Paradise: Marriage, Motherhood, and Women in Carolingian Edifying Literature.* New York, 1997.

Mirrer, Louise. *Upon My Husband's Death: Widows in the Literature and Histories of Medieval Europe.* Ann Arbor, 1992.

Mitchell, Linda E. *Women in Medieval Western European Culture.* New York, 1999.

Musacchio, Jacqueline M. *The Art and Ritual of Childbirth in Renaissance Italy.* New Haven, 1999.

Rousseau, Constance M., and Joel Rosenthal. *Women, Marriage, and the Family in Medieval Christendom* (honoring Michael Sheehan, CBS). Kalamazoo, 1998.

Swabey, Ffiona. *Medieval Gentlewoman: Life in a Widow's Household in the Later Middle Ages.* Gloucestershire, Sutton, 1999.

Uitz, Erika. *Die Frau in der Mittelalterlichen Stadt.* Freiburg, 1992.

Van Houts, Elizabeth. *Memory and Gender in Medieval Europe,* 900–1200. Basingstoke, Hampshire, 1999.

Walker, Sue Sheridan. *Wife and Widow in Medieval England.* Ann Arbor, 1993.

ON ROHEIS, HAWISIA, MARGARET, AND ELIZABETH:

Adams, Carol. *From Workshop to Warfare: The Lives of Medieval Women.* New York, 1983.

Bennett, Judith. *A Medieval Life: Cecilia Penifader of Brigstock, 1295–1344.* Boston, 1999.

———. *Sisters and Workers in the Middle Ages. Chicago, 1989.*

Bird, W. H. B., ed. *Calendar of the Close Rolls.* London, 1927'

Du Bruck, Edelgard E. *New Images of Medieval Women: Essays toward a Cultural Anthropology.* New York, 1989.

Echols, Anne, and Marty Williams. *An Annotated Index of Medieval Women.* New York, 1992

Edwards, Robert, and Vicki Ziegler. *Matrons and Marginal Women in Medieval Society.* Rochester, 1995.

Frankes, Jerold C. *Brides and Doom: Gender, Property, and Power in Medieval German Women's Epic.* Philadelphia, 1994.

Goldberg, P. J. P. *Woman Work, and the Life Cycle in a Medieval Economy: Women in York and Yorkshire, 1300–1520.* Oxford, 1992.

Howell, Martha C. *Women, Production, and Patriarchy in Late Medieval Cities.* Chicago, 1986.

Jewell, Helen. *Women in Medieval England.* New York, 1996.

Leyser, Henrietta. *Medieval Women: A Social History of Women in England, 450–1500.* New York, 1995.

Mate, Mavis. *Women in Medieval English Society.* New York, 1999.

Radcliffe-Umstead, Douglas. *Roles and Images of Women in the Middle Ages and Renaissance.* Pittsburgh, 1975.

Shahar, Shulamith. *The Fourth Estate: A History of Women in the Middle Ages.* Translated from the Hebrew by Chaya Galai. New York, 1990.

Sigler, Lora Ann. *The Genre of Gender: Images of Working Women in the Tacuina Sanitatis.* Los Angeles (UCLA Ph.D. thesis), 1992.

Williams, Marty. *Between Pit and Pedestal: Women in the Middle Ages.* Princeton, 1994.

DIRECTING CHURCH FACILITIES

ON WOMEN IN POWER IN THE CHURCH:

Bateson, Mary. "Origin and Early History of Double Monasteries." In *Transactions of the Royal Historical Society* n.s. 13 (1899): 137–198.

Bolton, Brenda. "Mulieres Sanctae." In *Women in Medieval Society,* edited by Susan Mosher Stuard. Philadelphia, 1976.

Brown, S., and J. O'Sullivan. *The Register of Eudes of Rouen.* New York, 1964.

Bynum, Caroline Walker. *Holy Feast and Holy Fast.* Berkeley, 1987.

Carpenter, Jennifer and Sally-Beth MacLean. *Power of the Weak: Studies on Medieval Women.* Urbana and Chicago, 1995.

Colledge, Eric. *The Medieval Mystics of England.* New York, 1961.

Collis, Louise. *Memoirs of a Medieval Woman: The Life and Times of Margery Kempe.* New York, 1964.

Dufournet, Jean; Pierre Toubert; Rita Lejeune; et al. *Femmes Mariage-Lignages xii–xiv siècles: Melanges offerts à Georges Duby.* Brussels, 1992.

Dronke, Peter. *Abelard and Heloise in Medieval Testimonies.* Totowa, N.J., 1977.

Eckenstein, Lina. *Woman under Monasticism.* Cambridge, 1896, 1922.

Ferrante, Joan M. *To the Glory of Her Sex: Women's Roles in the Composition of Medieval Texts.* Bloomington, 1997.

Godfrey, J. "The Double Monastery in Early English History." *AJ* 79 (1974): 19–32.

Gold, Penny Schine. *The Lady and the Virgin: Image, Attitude, and Experience in 12th-Century France.* Chicago, 1987.

Harrad of Landsburg. *Hortus Deliciarum, Facsimile by Caratzas Brothers.* New York, 1977.

Heinrich, Mary Pia. *The Canonesses and Education in the Early Middle Ages.* Washington, D.C., 1924.

Hentsch, Alice A. *De la littérature didactique du moyen age s'adressant spécialement aux femmes.* Geneva, 1975.

Herlihy, David. "Land, Family, and Women in Continental Europe." In *Women in Medieval Society,* edited by S. Stuard. Philadelphia, 1976.

Holloway, Julia B., Constance S. Wright, and Joan Bechtold. *Equally in God's Image: Women in the Middle Ages.* New York, 1990.

Leibell, Jane Frances, Sister. *Anglo-Saxon Education of Women: from Hilda to Hildegarde.* New York, 1971.

Lenzi, Maria Ludovica. *Donne e madonne: l'educazione femminile nel primo Rinascimento italiano.* Turin, 1982.

Lewis, Gertrud Jargon. *By Women, for Women, about Women: The Sister-Books of Fourteenth-Century Germany.* Toronto, 1996.

Lucas, Angela. *Women in the Middle Ages: Religion, Marriage, and Letters.* New York, 1983.

McLaughlin, Eleanor Commo. "Equality of Souls, Inequality of Sexes: Woman in Medieval Theology." In *Religion and Sexism: Images of Woman in the Jewish and Christian Traditions,* edited by Rosemary Radford Ruether. New York, 1974.

———. "Women, Power, and the Pursuit of Holiness in Medieval Christianity." In *Women of Spirit: Female Leadership in the Jewish and Christian Tradition,* edited by Rosemary Radford Ruether and Eleanor McLaughlin. New York, 1979.

McNamara, Jo Ann. "Sexual Equality and the Cult of Virginity in Early Christian Thought." *Feminist Studies* 3, 4 (Spring–Summer 1976): 144–58.

McNamara, Jo Ann, and Suzanne F. Wemple. "Sanctity and Power: The Dual Pursuit of Medieval Women." In *Becoming Visible: Women in European History,* edited by Renate Bridenthal and Claudia Koonz. Boston, 1974.

Morris, Joan. *The Lady Was a Bishop.* New York, 1973.

Nolan, Edward Peter. *Cry Out and Write: a Feminine Poetics of Revelation.* New York, 1994.

Parvey, Constance F. "The Theology and Leadership of Women in the New Testament." In *Religion and Sexism: Images of Woman in the Jewish and Christian Traditions,* edited by Rosemary Radford Ruether. New York, 1974.

Potkay, Monica Brzezinski, and Regula Meyer Evitt. *Minding the Body: Women and Literature in the Middle Ages, 800–1500.* London, New York, 1997.

Power, Eileen. *Medieval English Nunneries.* Cambridge, 1922.

Ruether, Rosemary. "Mothers of the Church: Ascetic Women in the Late Patristic Age." In *Women of Spirit: Female Leadership in the Jewish and Christian Traditions,* edited by Rosemary Ruether and Eleanor McLaughlin, New York, 1970.

———. "Virginal Feminism in the Fathers of the Church." In *Religion and Sexism: Images of Woman in the Jewish and Christian Traditions,* edited by Rosemary Radford Ruether. New York, 1974.

Ruether, Rosemary Radford, and Eleanor McLaughlin, eds. *Women of Spirit: Female Leadership in the Jewish and Christian Tradition.* New York, 1979.

Saxonhouse, Arlene W. *Women in the History of Political Thought.* New York, 1985.

Smith, Jacqueline. "Robert of Arbrissel: Procurator Mulierum." In *Medieval Women,* edited by Derek Baker. Oxford, 1978.

Wheeler, Bonnie. *Representations of the Feminine in the Middle Ages.* Dallas, 1993.

ON FONTEVRAULT:

Bateson, Mary. "Origin and Early History of Double Monasteries." In *Transactions of the Royal Historical Society* n.s. 13 (1899): 137–198.

Godfrey, J. "The Double Monastery in Early English History." *AJ* 79 (1974): 19–32.

Smith, Jacqueline. "Robert of Arbrissel: Procurator Mulierum." In *Medieval Women,* edited by Derek Baker. Oxford, 1978.

ON MARGERY KEMPE:

Collis, Louise. *Memoirs of a Medieval Woman: The Life and Times of Margery Kempe.* New York, 1964.

ON WOMEN MYSTICS:

Colledge, Eric. *The Medieval Mystics of England.* New York, 1961.

Collis, Louise. *Memoirs of a Medieval Woman: The Life and Times of Margery Kempe.* New York, 1964.

ON DOUBLE MONASTERIES:

Bateson, Mary. "Origin and Early History of Double Monasteries." In *Transactions of the Royal Historical Society* n.s. 13 (1899): 137–198.

Eckenstein, Lina. *Woman under Monasticism.* Cambridge, 1922.

Godfrey, J. "The Double Monastery in Early English History." *AJ* 79 (1974): 19–32.

Smith, Jacqueline. "Robert of Arbrissel: Procurator Mulierum." In *Medieval Women,* edited by Derek Baker. Oxford, 1978.

ON ABBESS HILDA OF WHITBY:

Of Northumbrian royalty, Hilda was baptized by Bishop Paulinus of York. She founded the double monastery of Whitby in 657. As abbess she hosted the powerful Synod of Whitby in 663 that attempted to reconcile liturgy and ecclesiastical usages of the English and Celts. Later canonized as Saint Hilda, her life was celebrated by The Venerable Bede in his *Ecclesiastical History of the English People.*

Bede. *Historia Ecclesiastica Gentis Anglorum.* Edited by T. Miller. London, 1890–1891.

Herbert, Kathleen. *Peace-Weavers and Shield-Maidens: Women in Early English Society.* Hockwold-cum-Wilton, 1997.

Leibell, Jane Frances, Sister. *Anglo-Saxon Education of Women: from Hilda to Hildegarde.* New York, 1971.

ON HELOISE OF ARGENTEUIL:

Dronke, Peter. *Abelard and Heloise in Medieval Testimonies.* Totowa, N.J., 1977.

Eckenstein, Lina. *Woman under Monasticism.* Cambridge, 1922.

ON ABBESS AND PHYSICIAN, HARRAD OF LANDSBURG:

Harrad of Landsberg. *Hortus Deliciarum.* Facsimile by Caratzas Brothers. New York, 1977.

ON EPISCOPAL POWER OF MEDIEVAL CHURCHWOMEN:

Amt, Emilie. *Women's Lives in Medieval Europe: A Sourcebook.* New York, 1993.

Ashley, Kathleen, and Paula Sheingorn. *Interpreting Cultural Symbols: Saint Anne in Late Medieval Society.* Athens, Ga., 1990.

Bennett, Judith. *Women in the Medieval Countryside: Gender and Household in Brigstock Before the Plague.* New York, 1987.

Blamires, Alcuin. *The Case for Women in Medieval Culture.* New York, 1997.

Bolton, Brenda. "Mulieres Sanctae." In *Women in Medieval Society,* edited by Susan M. Stuard. Philadelphia, 1976.

Bornstein, Daniel, and Roberto Rusconi. *Women and Religion in Medieval and Renaissance Italy.* Translated by M. Schneider. Chicago, 1996.

Bynum, Caroline Walker. *Fragmentation and Redemption: Essays on Gender and the Human Body in Medieval Religion.* Chicago, 1991.

Coon, Lynda L. *Sacred Fictions: Holy Women and Hagiography in Late Antiquity.* Philadelphia, 1997.

Elkins, Sharon. *Holy Women in Twelfth-Century England.* Chapel Hill, 1998.

Gilchrist, Roberta. *Contemplation and Action: The Other Monasticism.* London and New York, 1995.

Johnson, Penelope. *Equal in Monastic Profession: Religious Women in Medieval France.* Chicago, 1991.

Kerr, Benenice. *Religious Life for Women, 1100–1350: Fontevraud in England.* Oxford, 1999.

Makowski, Elizabeth. *Canon Law and Cloistered Women.* Washington, D.C., 1997.

Martin, Priscilla. *Chaucer's Women: Nuns, Wives and Amazons.* Houndmills, 1996.

McNamara, Jo Ann, and John E. Halborg. *Sainted Women of the Dark Ages.* Durham, 1992.

Morris, Joan. *The Lady Was a Bishop.* New York, 1973.

Morton, James. *The Nun's Rule. Being the Ancren Riwle Modernized.* New York, 1966.

Mundy, John Hine. *Men and Women in Toulouse in the Age of the Cathars.* Toronto, 1990.

Oliva, Marylin. *The Convent and the Community in Late Medieval England: Female Monastics in the Diocese of Norwich, 1350–1540.* Rochester, 1998.

Pardoe, Rosemary, and Darroll Pardoe. *The Female Pope: The Mystery of Pope Joan: The First Complete Documentation of Facts Behind the Legend.* New York, 1988.

Partner, Nancy F., *Studying Medieval Women: Sex, Gender, Feminism.* Cambridge, 1993.

Petroff, Elizabeth. *Body and Soul: Essays on Medieval Women and Monasticism.* New York, 1994.

Potkay, Monica Brzezinski, and Regula Meyer Evitt. *Minding the Body: Women and Literature in the Middle Ages, 800–1500.* London, New York, 1997.

Power, Eileen. *Medieval English Nunneries.* Cambridge, 1922.

Scarborough, Connie. *Women in Thirteenth-Century Spain as Portrayed in Alfonso X's Cantigas De Santa Maria.* Lewiston. 1993.

Schmitt, Miriam, and Linda Kulzer, eds. *Medieval Women Monastics: Wisdom's Wellsprings.* Collegeville, Minnesota, 1996.

Schulenberg, Jane Tibbetts. *Forgetful of Her Sex: Female Sanctity and Society, 500–1100.* Chicago, 1998.

Smith, Lesley, and Jane H. M. Taylor. *Women, the Book, and the Godly.* Rochester, 1995.

Thompson, Sally. *Women Religious: The Founding of English Nunneries after the Norman Conquest.* New York, 1991.

Tillotson, John. *Marrick Priory: A Nunnery in Late Medieval Yorkshire.* York, 1989.

Venarde, Bruce. *Women's Monasticism and Medieval Society: Nunneries in France and England, 890–1215.* Ithaca, 1997.

Watt, Diane. *Medieval Women in Their Communities.* Toronto and Buffalo, 1997.

Wood, Jeryldene. *Women, Art, and Spirituality: The Poor Clares of Early Modern Italy.* New York, 1996.

ON BISHOP EUDES'S VISITATIONS:

Brown, S., and J. O'Sullivan. *The Register of Eudes of Rouen.* New York, 1964.

Chapter 4

CRAFTSWOMEN: IN MARKETS, FIELDS, AND MINES

ON MEDIEVAL CRAFTSWOMEN:

Abrams, A. "Women Traders in Medieval London." *Economic Journal* 26 (1916): 276–285.

Arthur, Marylin B. "Early Greece: The Origins of the Western Attitude Toward Women." *Arethusa* 6 (Spring 1973).

Barber, Elizabeth. *Women's Work: The First 20,000 Years.* New York, 1994.

Beardwood, Alice. *Alien Merchants in England, 1355–77.* Cambridge, 1931.

Boissonade, P. *Life and Work in Medieval Europe: The Evolution of Medieval Economy from the Fifth to the Fifteenth Centuries.* Translated by Eileen Power. New York, 1964.

Branca, Vittore. *Mercanti scrittori.* Milan, 1986.

Braudel, Fernand. *Capitalism and the Material Life.* Translated by M. Kochas. New York, 1973.

Bridenthal, Renate and Claudia Koonz. *Becoming Visible: Women in European History.* Boston, 1974.

NOTES AND REFERENCES

Carus-Wilson, E. M. *Medieval Merchant Adventurers.* London, 1967.

Clark, Alice. The Working Life of Women in the 17th Century. London, 1919.

Cosman, Madeleine Pelner. "A Chicken for Chaucer's Kitchen: Medieval London's Market Laws and Larcenies." In *Fabulous Feasts, Medieval Cookery and Ceremony.* New York, 1976, 1998.

———. *The Medieval Baker's Daughter.* Tenafly, 1984.

———. *Medieval Holidays and Festivals: A Calendar of Celebrations.* New York, London, 1981.

———. *Medieval WordBook.* New York, 1996.

———. *Fabulous Feasts: Medieval Cookery and Ceremony.* New York, 1976, 1998.

Cosman, Madeleine Pelner, and Bruce Chandler, eds. *Machaut's World: Science and Art in the Fourteenth Century.* New York, 1978.

Dale, M. K. "The London Silk Women of the 15th Century." *Economic History Review* 4: 324–35.

English, Edward. *Enterprise and Liability in Sienese Banking 1230–1350.* Cambridge, 1988.

Goitein, Samuel D. *A Mediterranean Society: the Jewish Communities of the Arab World as Portrayed in the Documents of the Cairo Geniza.* Berkeley, 1967, 1971.

———. *Letters of Medieval Jewish Traders.* Princeton, 1973.

Hanawalt, Barbara. *Women and Work in Pre-Industrial Europe.* Bloomington, 1986.

Harksen, Sibylle. *La Femme au Moyen-Age.* Leipzig, 1974; translated as *Women in the Middle Ages.* New York and London, 1975.

Harris, A. S. and L. Nochlin. *Women Artists: 1550–1950.* New York, 1977.

Hays, H. R. *The Dangerous Sex: The Myth of Feminine Evil.* New York, 1964.

Heer, Friedrich. *The Medieval World.* Translated by Janet Sondheimer. New York, 1962.

Henry, Sondra and Emily Taitz. *Written Out of History: A Hidden Legacy of Jewish Women Revealed Through Their Writings and Letters.* New York, 1978.

Herlihy, David. "Land, Family, and Women in Continental Europe, 701–1200." In *Women in Medieval Society,* edited by Susan Mosher Stuard. Philadelphia, 1976, pp. 13–45.

———. *Women in Medieval Society.* Houston, 1971.

———. *Medieval and Renaissance Pistoia.* New Haven, 1967.

———. "Life Expectancies of Medieval Women." In *The Role of Women in the Middle Ages,* edited by Rosemarie Morewedge. Albany, 1975.

———. *Opera Muliebria: Women and Work in Medieval Europe.* New York, 1990.

Holloway, Julia B; Constance S. Wright; and Joan Bechtold. *Equally in God's Image: Women in the Middle Ages.* New York, 1990.

Howell, Martha. *Women, Production, and Patriarchy in Late Medieval Cities.* Chicago, 1986.

Janeway, Elizabeth. *Man's World, Woman's Place.* New York, 1971.

Jordan, William C. *Women and Credit in Pre-Industrial and Developing Societies.* Philadelphia, 1993.

Katzenellenbogen, A. *Allegories of the Virtues and Vices in Medieval Art.* London, 1939.

Kedar, Benjamin. *Merchants in Crisis: Genoese and Venetian Men of Affairs and the 14th-Century Depression.* New Haven, 1976.

Kirschner, Julius and Suzanne Wemple, eds. *Women of the Medieval World.* Oxford, 1985.

Lane, Frederic. *Andreas Barbarigo, Merchant of Venice.* New York, 1967.

Laslett, P., and R. Wald. *Household and Family in Past Time.* Cambridge, 1972.

Le Goff, Jacques. *Time, Work, and Culture in the Middle Ages.* Translated by Arthur Goldhammer. Chicago, 1980.

————. *Medieval Callings.* Translated by Lydia Cochrane. Chicago, 1987.

————. *Your Money or Your Life: La Bourse et la vie.* Translated by Patricia Ranum. New York, 1988.

Lopez, Robert. *The Commercial Revolution of the Middle Ages.* Cambridge, 1976.

Lopez, Robert, and Irving Raymond. *Medieval Trade in the Mediterranean World.* New York and London, 1968.

Mate, Mavis E. *Daughters, Wives, and Widows After the Black Death: Women in Sussex 1350–1535.* Woodbridge, U.K., and Rochester, N.Y., 1998.

Nicholas, David. *The Domestic Life of a Medieval City: Women, Children and the Family in 14th-Century Ghent.* Lincoln, 1985.

Origo, Iris. *The Merchant of Prato.* Boston, 1986.

Postan, M. M. *Medieval Trade and Finance.* Cambridge, 1973.

Power, Eileen. *The Medieval English Wool Trade.* London, 1941.

————. *Medieval Women.* Edited by M. M. Postan. Cambridge, 1975.

Reynouard, Yves. *Les hommes d'affaires italiens du Moyen Age.* Edited by Bernard Guillemain. Paris, 1968.

de Roover, Raymond. *Money, Banking, and Credit in Medieval Bruges.* Cambridge, 1948.

Ryerson, Kathryn. *Business, Banking, and Finance in Medieval Montpellier.* Toronto, 1985.

Samuel, Edgar. "Was Moyse's Hall, Bury St. Edmunds, a Jew's House?" *The Jewish Historical Society of England Transactions:* 25, Miscellanies X, 1977.

Sapori, Armando. *The Italian Merchant in the Middle Ages.* Translated by Patricia Anne Kennen. New York, 1970.

Shahar, Shulamith. *The Fourth Estate: A History of Women in the Middle Ages.* New York, 1983.

Thrupp, Sylvia. *The Merchant Class of Medieval London.* Ann Arbor, 1962.

Vittore, Branca. *Mercanti scrittori.* Milan, 1986.

ON MEDIEVAL MARRIAGE:

Bynum, Caroline Walker. *Holy Feast and Holy Fast: The Religious Significance of Food to Medieval Women.* Berkeley, 1987.

Duby, Georges. *The Knight, the Lady and the Priest: The Making of Modern Marriage in Medieval France.* Translated by Barbara Bray. New York, 1984.

Dufournet, Jean; Pierre Toubert; Rita Lejeune; et al. *Femmes, Mariage-Lignages xii–xiv siècles: Melanges offerts à Georges Duby.* Brussels, 1992.

Falk, Ze'ev W. *Jewish Matrimonial Law in the Middle Ages.* Oxford, 1966.

Gies, Frances, and Joseph Gies. *Marriage and the Family in the Middle Ages.* New York, 1987.

Gold, Penny Schine. *The Lady and the Virgin: Image, Attitude, and Experience in 12th-Century France.* Chicago, 1987.

Goody, Jack. *The Development of the Family and Marriage in Europe.* New York, 1983.

Herlihy, David. *Medieval Households.* Cambridge, 1985.

———. "Life Expectancies of Medieval Women." In *The Role of Women in the Middle Ages,* edited by Rosemarie Morewedge. Albany, 1975.

Holloway, Julia B, Constance S. Wright, and Joan Bechtold. *Equally in God's Image: Women in the Middle Ages.* New York, 1990.

Klapisch-Zuber, Christiane. "Women and the Family." In *Medieval Callings,* edited by Jacques Le Goff. Chicago, 1990.

Laslett, P., and R. Wald. *Household and Family in Past Time.* Cambridge, 1972.

Lyerle, John, ed. *Marriage in the Middle Ages. Viator* 4 (1973).

Mate, Mavis E. *Daughters, Wives, and Widows After the Black Death: Women in Sussex 1350–1535.* Woodbridge, U.K., and Rochester, N.Y., 1998.

Nicholas, David. *The Domestic Life of a Medieval City: Women, Children and the Family in 14th-Century Ghent.* Lincoln, 1985.

Stafford, Pauline. *Queens, Concubines, and Dowagers: The King's Wife in the Early Middle Ages.* New York, 1983.

FABRIC TRADESWOMEN

(*See* SILK AND WOOL CRAFTSWOMEN)

FOOD TRADESWOMEN

ON THE ASSIZE OF BREAD:

In the "moldingborde" scam of 1327 two baxters named Alice de Brightenoch and Lucy de Pykering plus eight men bakers were found guilty of owning and using fraudulent moldingbordes. Those in possession of moldingbordes plus stolen dough were punished more harshly than their colleagues possessing only equipment, not contraband product. The baxters were punished with the lesser penalty of time in Newgate Prison while men possessing stolen dough were punished by exposure on the pillory with a quantity of pilfered dough strung on a rope hung from their necks "until Vespers at St. Paul ended."

The Latin document from the reign of King Edward III comes from the London Guildhall's bread court memoranda:

Assisa Panis, Folio 79 B, also mentioned in the Liber Albus, 289 A.

This case is central to a bilingual children's book used in schools nationwide in states with high percentages of Spanish-speaking students. Originally it was written for New York City's School District Six, home to The Cloisters, the medieval museum of the Metropolitan Museum of Art.

Cosman, Madeleine Pelner. *The Medieval Baker's Daughter: La Hija de la Panadera Medieval.* Tenafly, N.J. 1984.
Ashley, Sir William. *The Bread of Our Forefathers: An Inquiry in Economic History.* London, 1828.
Thrupp, Sylvia. *A Short History of the Worshipful Company of Bakers of London.* London, 1933.

ON THE ALE-WIFE AND HER FALSE MEASURE:

The Latin court case dates from the reign of King Edward III.

Letter Book G, Folio 137 (1364).
Bennett, Judith. *Ale, Beer, and Brewsters in England.* New York, 1996.

ON MISERICORDS:

Bond, Francis. *Wood Carving in English Churches:* I. Misericords; II. Stalls. London, 1910.
Kraus, Dorothy and Henry Kraus. *The Hidden World of Misericords.* New York, 1975.
Remnant, G. L. *A Catalogue of Misericords in Great Britain.* London, 1969.

ON MARJORIE HORE, THE "FISSHWYFE":

She was punished on the thewe for endangering public health by selling stinking soles. The Latin document dates from the reign of King Edward III, 1372.

Letter Book G, Folio 292

MATRONYMICS

ON MATRONYMICS AND THE CLERICAL OR "NICHOLAITE" FAMILIES:

Herlihy, David. "Land, Family, and Women in Continental Europe, 701–1200." In *Women in Medieval Society,* edited by Susan Mosher Stuard. Philadelphia, 1976.

LAW, DEMOGRAPHY, AND PERSONAL VALUE

ON WOMEN'S "WORTH":

Bullough, Vern. *The Subordinate Sex: A History of Attitudes Towards Women.* Urbana, 1973.

———. "Medieval Medical and Scientific Views of Women." In *Marriage in the Middle Ages,* edited by John Lyerle, *Viator* 4 (1973).

Herlihy, David. "Life Expectancies of Medieval Women." In *The Role of Women in the Middle Ages,* edited by Rosemarie Morewedge. Albany, 1975.

———. "Land, Family, and Women in Continental Europe, 701–1200." In *Women in Medieval Society,* edited by Susan Mosher Stuard. Philadelphia, 1976.

Rivers, Theodore John. *Laws of the Alamans and Bavarians.* Philadelphia, 1977.

Russell, Josiah Cox. *Late Ancient and Medieval Population.* Philadelphia, 1958.

Wrigley, E. A. *Population and History.* New York, 1969.

ON MEDIEVAL CONTRACEPTION AND ABORTION:

Boswell, John. *Christianity, Social Tolerance, and Homosexuality.* Chicago, 1980.

Bullough, Vern. *The Subordinate Sex: A History of Attitudes Towards Women.* Urbana, 1973.

———. "Medieval Medical and Scientific Views of Women." In *Marriage in the Middle Ages,* edited by John Lyerle, *Viator* 4 (1973).

———. "Sex Education in Medieval Christianity." *The Journal of Sex Research* 13 (1977): 185–96.

Coleman, Emily. "Infanticide in the Early Middle Ages." In *Women in Medieval Society,* edited by Susan M. Stuard. Philadelphia, 1976.

Cosman, Madeleine Pelner. "Criminalization of Abortion Knowledge." A review of John Riddle's *Eve's Herbs: A History of Contraception and Abortion in the West. Journal of the American Medical Association,* January 1998.

———. "Regulating Childbirth in Medical Law History." A review of John M. Riddle's *Contraception and Abortion from the Ancient World to the Renaissance. Journal of the American Medical Association,* May 1995.

———. "Medical Law and the Renaissance Discovery of the Clitoris." A review of F. Andehazi's *The Anatomist. Journal of the American Medical Association,* August 1999.

———. "Criminalization of Women and Trials of Witches." A review of Helen Rodnite Lemay's *Women's Secrets, Pseudo-Albertus Magnus' De Secretum Mulieris. Journal of the History of Medicine and Allied Sciences,* March 1994.

Forbes, Thomas. *The Midwife and the Witch.* New Haven, 1961.

Hanawalt, Barbara. "The Female Felon in 14th-Century England." In *Women in Medieval Society,* edited by Susan M. Stuard. Philadelphia, 1976.

Himes, N. E. *A Medical History of Contraception.* Baltimore, 1936.

Le Goff, Jacques. "Licit and Illicit Trades in the Medieval West." *In Time, Work, and Culture in the Middle Ages,* translated by Arthur Goldhammer. Chicago, 1980.

Lemay, Helen Rodnite. *Women's Secrets, Pseudo-Albertus Magnus' De Secretum Mulieris*. Albany, 1992.

McLaren, Angus. *A History of Contraception from Antiquity to the Present Day*. London, 1990.

Miller, B. D. H. "She who hath drunk any potion." *Medium Aevum* 31 (1962): 188–193.

Noonan, John. *Contraception*. Cambridge, 1965.

Riddle, John. *Eve's Herbs: A History of Contraception and Abortion in the West*. Cambridge, 1997.

———. *Contraception and Abortion from the Ancient World to the Renaissance*. Cambridge, 1992.

Thrupp, Sylvia. *The Merchant Class of Medieval London*. Ann Arbor, 1962.

SILK AND WOOL CRAFTSWOMEN

ON LONDON SILKWOMEN:

Abrams, A. "Women Traders in Medieval London." *Economic Journal* 26 (1916): 276–285.

Beardwood, Alice. *Alien Merchants in England, 1355–77*. Cambridge, 1931.

Dale, M. K. "The London Silk Women of the 15th Century." *Economic History Review* 4: 324–35.

Postan, M. M. *Medieval Trade and Finance*. Cambridge, 1973.

ON ROSE OF BURFORD, WOOL MERCHANT:

Calendar of Plea and Memoranda Rolls of the City of London 1323–1364. Edited by R. R. Sharpe. London, 1899.

Calendar of Wills in the Court of Husting. Edited by R. R. Sharpe. London, 1899, I: 238.

Issues of the Exchequer. Edited by F. Devon. London, 1937. 133.

Power, Eileen. *Medieval Women*. Edited by M. M. Postan. Cambridge, 1975.

———. *The Medieval English Wool Trade*. London, 1941.

Rotuli Hundredorum tempore Henry III, Edward I. I: 403. London, 1818.

JEWISH CRAFTSWOMEN

ON JEWISH WOMEN BROKERS AND THE LETTER FROM DAVID MAIMONIDES:

The letter is preserved at Cambridge University in the University Library as Manuscript OR 1081 J 1; Professor Goitein has translated it and published it as his Letter 42.

Goitein, Samuel D. *Letters of Medieval Jewish Traders*. Princeton, 1973.

He lists other Geniza references to medieval Jewish women brokers I: 532, index; II, 419, sec. 36; II, 481, sec. 30.

Goitein, Samuel D. *A Mediterranean Society: the Jewish Communities of the Arab World as Portrayed in the Documents of the Cairo Geniza.* Berkeley, 1967, 1971.

ON JEWISH WOMEN PROPERTY OWNERS
OF BURY ST. EDMUNDS:

Samuel, Edgar. "Was Moyse's Hall, Bury St. Edmunds, a Jew's House?" *The Jewish Historical Society of England Transactions:* 25, Miscellanies X (1977).

ON OTHER JEWISH BUSINESSWOMEN, SUCH AS
14TH-CENTURY GRACIA MENDES:

Baer, Yitzak. *A History of the Jews in Christian Spain.* Philadelphia, 1966.
Carpenter, Jennifer and Sally Beth MacLean. *Power of the Weak: Studies on Medieval Women.* Urbana and Chicago, 1995.
Falk, Ze'ev W. *Jewish Matrimonial Law in the Middle Ages.* Oxford, 1966.
Henry, Sondra and Emily Taitz. *Written Out of History: A Hidden Legacy of Jewish Women Revealed Through Their Writings and Letters.* New York, 1978.
Netanyahu, B. *The Marranos of Spain from the Late XIVth to the Early XVIth Century.* New York, 1966.

WEALTHY WIDOWED CRAFTSWOMEN

ON ELIZABETH KYRKEBY, THE RICH WIDOW:

The 15th-century draper claimed her fortune by alleging he had a marriage contract with Elizabeth Kyrkeby, widowed at John Kyrkeby's death in 1484. Professor Thrupp provides the amusing list of the draper's gifts to Elizabeth and their costs.

Letter Book L, Folio 216 (1484).
Thrupp, Sylvia. *The Merchant Class of Medieval London,* 107. Ann Arbor, 1962.

ON THE KUTNA HORA SILVER MINES:

For introducing me to the women miners of Kutna Hora, and for his congenial help in reviewing legal documents, art photos, and metallurgical treatises relevant to mining in medieval Hungary, I am grateful to Dr. George Szabo, who during the time we worked together was the curator of the Lehmann Collection of the Metropolitan Museum of Art and distinguished visiting professor at the Institute for Medieval and Renaissance Studies, City College of City University of New York.

Chapter 5

WOMEN IN ILLICIT TRADES

ON WOMEN IN THE ILLICIT TRADES:

Bellamy, John. *Crime and Public Order in England in the Later Middle Ages.* Toronto, 1973.

Boswell, John. *The Kindness of Strangers: The Abandonment of Children in Western Europe from Late Antiquity to the Renaissance.* New York, 1988.

————. *Christianity, Social Tolerance, and Homosexuality.* Chicago, 1980.

Bullough, Vern. *Sexual Variance in Society and History.* New York, 1976.

————. *The Subordinate Sex: A History of Attitudes Towards Women.* Urbana, 1973.

————. "Medieval Medical and Scientific Views of Women," *Marriage in the Middle Ages,* edited by John Lyerle. *Viator* 4 (1973).

————. *The History of Prostitution.* New Hyde Park, 1964.

————. "Sex Education in Medieval Christianity." In *The Journal of Sex Research* 13 (1977): 185–96.

Chazan, Robert. *Daggers of Faith: Thirteenth-Century Christian Missionizing and the Jewish Response.* Berkeley, 1989.

Cohn, Norman. *The Pursuit of the Millennium.* New York, 1970.

Coleman, Emily. "Infanticide in the Early Middle Ages." In *Women in Medieval Society,* edited by Susan M. Stuard. Philadelphia, 1976.

Cosman, Madeleine Pelner. "Criminalization of Abortion Knowledge." A review of John Riddle's *Eve's Herbs: A History of Contraception and Abortion in the West. Journal of the American Medical Association,* January 1998.

————. "Criminalization of Women and Trials of Witches." A review of Helen Rodnite Lemay's *Women's Secrets, Pseudo-Albertus Magnus' De Secretum Mulieris. Journal of the History of Medicine and Allied Sciences,* March 1994.

————. "Medical Law and the Renaissance Discovery of the Clitoris." A review of F. Andehazi's *The Anatomist. Journal of the American Medical Association,* August 1999.

————. "Medieval Medical Malpractice: The Dicta and the Dockets." In *Bulletin of the New York Academy of Medicine* 49, 1 (1973): 22–47.

————. "Regulating Childbirth in Medical Law History." A review of John M. Riddle's *Contraception and Abortion from the Ancient World to the Renaissance. Journal of the American Medical Association,* May 1995.

————. "Sex, Smut, Sin, and Spirit." In *Fabulous Feasts: Medieval Cookery and Ceremony.* New York, 1976, 1978, 1998.

Duby, Georges. *Medieval Marriage, Two Models from 12th-Century France.* Translated by Elborg Forster. Baltimore, 1978.

Edwards, Robert, and Vickie Ziegler. *Matrons and Marginal Women in Medieval Society.* Rochester, 1995.

Forbes, Thomas. *The Midwife and the Witch.* New Haven, 1961.

Geremek, Bronislaw. *The Margins of Paris. Les marginaux parisiens aux XIVe et XVe siècles.* Translated by Jean Birrell. New York, 1987.

Given, James Buchanan. *Society and Homicide in Thirteenth-Century England.* Stanford, 1977.

Grillot de Givry, E. *Witchcraft, Magic, and Alchemy.* New York, 1971. Originally called *Illustrated Anthology of Sorcery, Magic, and Alchemy.* Chicago, 1958.

Gross, C. "Modes of Trial in the Medieval Boroughs of England." *Harvard Law Review* 15 (1901–1902): 695–701.

Hanawalt, Barbara. *Crime and Conflict in English Communities: 1300–1348.* Cambridge, 1979.

———. "The Female Felon in 14th-Century England." In *Women in Medieval Society,* edited by Susan M. Stuard. Philadelphia, 1976.

Hanawalt Westman, Barbara. "The Peasant Family and Crime in Fourteenth Century England." In *Journal of British Studies* 13 (1974).

———. *A Study of Crime in Norfolk, Yorkshire, and Northamptonshire 1300–1348.* Doctoral thesis. University of Michigan, 1970.

Hilton, R. H. *Bond Men Made Free: Medieval Peasant Movements and the English Rising of 1381.* New York, 1973.

Himes, N. E. *A Medical History of Contraception.* Baltimore, 1936.

Jusserand, J. J. *English Wayfaring Life in the Middle Ages.* London, 1961.

Kramer, H., and J. Sprenger. *Malleus Maleficarum.* 1487; *The Hammer of Witches.* Translated by M. Summers. London, 1928.

Ladner, Gerhart. "Homo Viator: Medieval Ideas on Alienation and Order." *Speculum* 42 (1967): 233–259.

Le Goff, Jacques. "Licit and Illicit Trades in the Medieval West." In *Time, Work, and Culture in the Middle Ages,* translated by Arthur Goldhammer. Chicago, 1980.

Lemay, Helen Rodnite. *Women's Secrets, Pseudo-Albertus Magnus' De Secretum Mulieris.* Albany, 1992.

Mannheim, H. *Comparative Criminology.* Boston, 1967.

McLaren, Angus. *A History of Contraception from Antiquity to the Present Day.* London, 1990.

Meek, Christine, and Katherine Simms. *'The Frailty of Her Sex'? Medieval Irishwomen in Their European Context.* Dublin, 1996.

Miller, B. D. H. "She who hath drunk any potion." *Medium Aevum.* 31 (1962): 188–193.

Moore, R. I. *The Formation of a Persecuting Society: Power and Deviance in Western Europe.* Oxford, 1987.

Noonan, John. *Contraception.* Cambridge, 1965.

Otis, Leah Lydia. *Prostitution in Medieval Society: The History of an Urban Institution in Languedoc.* Chicago, 1985.

Pike, L. O. *History of Crime in England.* London, 1873.

Pollock, O. *The Criminality of Women.* Philadelphia, 1950.

Riddle, John. *Eve's Herbs: A History of Contraception and Abortion in the West.* Cambridge, 1997.

——. *Contraception and Abortion from the Ancient World to the Renaissance.* Cambridge, 1992.

Riley, H. T. *Memorials of London and London Life.* London, 1868.

Rubens, Alfred. *A History of Jewish Costume.* London, 1973.

Stenton, Doris May. *Rolls of the Justices in Eyre . . . 1221, 1222.* London, 1940.

——. *Pleas Before the King or His Justices 1198–1212.* London, 1952–1967.

Tierney, Brian. *Medieval Poor Law: A Sketch of Canonical Theory and its Application in England.* Berkeley, 1959.

Vicellio, Cesare. *Habiti Antici di Tutti il Mondo.* Venice, 1590. Published by Dover as *Vicellio's Renaissance Costume Book.* New York, 1977.

Williams, Marty and Anne Echols. *Between Pit and Pedestal: Women in the Middle Ages.* Princeton, 1994.

PROSTITUTES

ON LONDON'S REGULATION OF SEX NEIGHBORHOODS IN THE 14TH CENTURY:

Norman French documents dating from the reigns of King Edward III and King Richard II:

Letter Book F, Folio 208 (1351).
Letter Book H, Folio 139 (1382).
Letter Book H, Folio 287 (1393).

ON SUMPTUARY LAW:

Baldwin, F. E. *Sumptuary Legislation and Personal Regulation in England.* Baltimore, 1926.

ON REGULATION AND ILLUSTRATION OF EUROPEAN PROSTITUTES' GARB:

Baldwin, F. E. *Sumptuary Legislation and Personal Regulation in England.* Baltimore, 1926.

Vicellio, Cesare. *Habiti Antici di Tutti il Mondo.* Venice, 1590. Published by Dover as *Vicellio's Renaissance Costume Book.* New York, 1977.

ON AN ORDINANCE OF KING HENRY V AGAINST THE "STEWS":

This document concludes with a "savings clause" permitting personal heated baths for one's private enjoyment.

Letter Book I, Folio 193 (1417).

ON THE HARLOT-HOUSEKEEPER:
Court Rolls of the Manor of Wakefield. Edited by W. P. Baildon, et al. 57: 94–95 (1901–1945).

ON WHORE LORE IN FOLKLORE AND NURSERY RHYMES:
Barchilon, Jacques, and Henry Pettit. *The Authentic Mother Goose.* Denver, 1960.
Baring-Gould, William. *The Annotated Mother Goose.* London, 1962.
Delamar, Gloria. *Mother Goose from Nursery to Literature.* Jefferson, N. C., and London, 1987.
Opie, Iona, and Peter Opie. *The Oxford Dictionary of Nursery Rhymes.* London, 1951.
Stith Thompson. *Motif-Index of Folk-Literature: a Classification of Narrative Elements in Folktale . . . Medieval Romances . . . Fabliaux.* Bloomington, 1932–36; computer file, CD-ROM, Bloomington, 1993.
Wimberly, Lowry. *Folklore in the English and Scottish Ballads.* New York, 1959.

ON ELIZABETH, THE EMBROIDERER-MADAM:
Letter Book H, Folio 194 (1385).

ON VIOLA'S ADVENTURES:
Her exuberant tale is one of 50 15th-century Italian novellas by Masuccio Salernitano, also known as Tommaso Guardato di Salerno. Printed in a 19th-century Italian edition, it is cherished by Chaucer students in the superbly translated bilingual edition by Benson and Andersson.

Benson, Larry D., and Theodore Andersson. *The Literary Context of Chaucer's Fabliaux.* Indianapolis, New York, 1971.
Masuccio Salernitano. *Novellino.* 1476.
Settembrini, Luigi. *Novellino: restituto alla sua antica lezione.* Naples, 1874.

ON PROSTITUTION'S WAXING AND WANING:
Bullough, Vern. *The History of Prostitution.* New Hyde Park, 1964.
Duby, Georges. *Rural Economy and Country Life in the Medieval West.* London and Columbia, 1968.
Otis, Leah Lydia. *Prostitution in Medieval Society: The History of an Urban Institution in Languedoc.* Chicago, 1985.
Postan, M. M. "Medieval Agrarian Society at its Prime, England." In *Cambridge Economic History of Europe,* edited by M. M. Postan. Cambridge, 1966.
Riddle, John. *Contraception and Abortion from the Ancient World to the Renaissance.* Cambridge, 1992.
———. *Eve's Herbs: A History of Contraception and Abortion in the West.* Cambridge, 1997.

Russell, Josiah Cox. *Late Ancient and Medieval Population*. Philadelphia, 1958.
Wrigley, E. A. *Population and History*. New York, 1969.

MURDERERS

ON WOMEN'S CRIMINALITY TANGENTIALLY RELATED TO LAW AND HEALTH:

While studying medical malpractice and public health documents I encountered women market malefactors in documents of London's Assize of Bread and its Assize of Ale, the medieval market courts, whose larcenies posed dangers to public health.

Some legal cases relating trials and punishments for false measurements introduced malefactors who endangered not the populace's health but commerce. False scales underweighing produce or false liquid measures decanting too little precious fluid for amount paid aided merchants' intentional misrepresentation of material fact upon which the populace detrimentally depended. Women and men market frauds in 14th-century London included "hucksters," or retailers using a false measure called a *chopyn*. During the reign of King Edward III, Alice Hurle, Agnes Damas, Johanna Hanel, Cristina atte Felde, Elena, Cecily, and others were convicted of using the *chopyn* and were punished.

Letter Book G, Folio 258 (1370).
Cosman, Madeleine Pelner. "A Chicken for Chaucer's Kitchen." In *Fabulous Feasts: Medieval Cookery and Ceremony*. New York 1976, 1978, 1998.

Adjacent to a document of critical medico-legal interest I found documents of more general felonious import, such as a Latin record of a trial during the reign of King Edward III for theft and the punishment by hanging of Desiderata de Toryntone. She had stolen 30 dishes and 24 saltcellars and was apprehended red-handed, with 14 dishes and 12 salts on her person.

Letter Book E, Folio 241 (1337).

Excellent studies of women's criminality in historical context:

Bellamy, John. *Crime and Public Order in England in the Later Middle Ages*. Toronto, 1973.
Hanawalt, Barbara. *Crime and Conflict in English Communities: 1300–1348*. Cambridge, 1979.
———. "The Female Felon in 14th-Century England." In *Women in Medieval Society*, edited by Susan M. Stuard. Philadelphia, 1976.

Hanawalt Westman, Barbara. "The Peasant Family and Crime in Fourteenth Century England." *Journal of British Studies* 13:2 (1974).
———. *A Study of Crime in Norfolk, Yorkshire, and Northamptonshire, 1300–1348.* Doctoral thesis, University of Michigan, 1970.
Pike, L. O. *History of Crime in England.* London, 1873.
Pollock, O. *The Criminality of Women.* Philadelphia, 1950.

ON ALICE GRUT AND ALICE GRYM:

London Public Record Office books of the Justice Itinerant III for the years 1300–1348 at 48 m. 4d.
Hanawalt, Barbara. "The Female Felon in 14th-Century England." In *Women in Medieval Society,* edited by Susan M. Stuard. Philadelphia, 1976.

ON ROBERT CULLINGWORTH AND THOMAS DAREL:

London Public Record Office books of the Justice Itinerant III for the years 1300–1348 at 77 2 m. 3.
London Public Record Office books of the Justice Itinerant III for the years 1300–1348 at 48 m. 4d. And at 75 m. 13–16.

ON THE *VICTIM'S* INSANITY THAT REQUIRED HER MURDERING HIM LEST HE MURDER HER:

Bedfordshire Coroners' Rolls. 16:102, edited by R. F. Hunnisett. Bedfordshire, 1960.
Robinson, Daniel N. *Wild Beasts and Idle Humours: The Insanity Defense from Antiquity to the Present.* Cambridge, 1996.

ON INFANTICIDE:

Boserup, E. *Conditions of Agricultural Growth.* Chicago, 1965.
Coleman, Emily. "Infanticide in the Early Middle Ages." In *Women in Medieval Society,* edited by Susan M. Stuard. Philadelphia, 1976.
Godefroy, L. "Infanticide." *Dictionnaire de théologie catholique.* Paris 1923. 7:2:1717–1726.
Himes, N. E. *A Medical History of Contraception.* Baltimore, 1936.
McLaren, Angus. *A History of Contraception from Antiquity to the Present Day.* London, 1990.
Miller, B. D. H. "She who hath drunk any potion." *Medium Aevum* 31 (1962): 188–193.
Noonan, John. *Contraception.* Cambridge, 1965.
Pentikaien, J. *The Nordic Dead-Child Tradition.* Helsinki, 1968.
Russell, Josiah Cox. *Late Ancient and Medieval Population.* Philadelphia, 1958.
Wrigley, E. A. *Population and History.* New York, 1969.

ON THE INSANITY PLEAS OF AGNES, MATILDE, AND MARJORIE:

Hanawalt, Barbara. "The Female Felon in 14th-Century England." In *Women in Medieval Society,* edited by Susan M. Stuard. Philadelphia, 1976.

Hanawalt Westman, Barbara. "The Peasant Family and Crime in Fourteenth Century England," *Journal of British Studies* 13:2 (1974).

———. *A Study of Crime in Norfolk, Yorkshire, and Northamptonshire 1300–1348.* Doctoral thesis. University of Michigan, 1970.

Robinson, Daniel N. *Wild Beasts and Idle Humours: The Insanity Defense from Antiquity to the Present.* Cambridge, 1996.

ON THE MEDIEVAL CULTURAL CONTEXT FOR MADNESS:

Madness included the disease called lovesickness or *hereos.* Odd, "crazy," "masochistic," and self-destructive behaviors were seen as punishment, purgation, expiation of sin, proof of holiness, or, paradoxically, imitations of Jesus Christ's stigmata and sufferings.

Bell, Rudolph M. *Holy Anorexia.* Chicago, 1985.

Bynum, Caroline Walker. *Holy Feast and Holy Fast.* Berkeley, 1987.

Doob, Penelope B. R. *Nebuchadnezzar's Children: Conventions of Madness in Middle English Literature.* New Haven, 1974.

Jackson, Stanley. *Melancholia and Depression from Hippocratic Times to Modern Times.* Yale, 1986.

Wack, Mary. *Lovesickness in the Middle Ages: The Viaticum and its Commentaries.* Philadelphia, 1990.

ON THE CANTILUPE LOVE KILLING IN 1375:

Records of Some Sessions of the Peace in Lincolnshire, 1360–1375. Edited by R. Sillem for the Lincoln Record Society. London, 1936.

ON MARJORIE BEREWICK:

London Public Record Office books of the Justice Itinerant III for the years 1300–1348 at 48 m. 32.

Hanawalt, Barbara. "The Female Felon in 14th-Century England." In *Women in Medieval Society,* edited by Susan M. Stuard. Philadelphia, 1976.

ON MATHILDE HERREWARD OF BRANNESDESTON:

London Public Record Office books of the Kings Bench 27, 322 m. 32.

Hanawalt, Barbara. "The Female Felon in 14th-Century England." In *Women in Medieval Society,* edited by Susan M. Stuard. Philadelphia, 1976.

THIEVES AND MARKET LAWBREAKERS
ON ALICE GARLIC:
London Public Record Office books of the Justice Itinerant III for the years 1300–1348 at 48 m. 22.

ON THE "MOLDINGBORDE" SCAM OF 1327:
The Latin document from the reign of King Edward III comes from the London Guildhall's bread court memoranda.

Assisa Panis, Folio 79 B, also mentioned in Liber Albus, 289 A.

Two baxters named Alice de Brightenoch and Lucy de Pykering and eight male bakers were found guilty of owning and using fraudulent "moldingbordes." Those possessing stolen dough were punished more harshly than their colleagues possessing only equipment, not contraband product. The baxters were punished with the lesser penalty of time in Newgate prison while those men possessing stolen dough were punished by exposure on the pillory with a quantity of pilfered dough hung from a rope around their necks "until Vespers at St. Paul ended."

This case is central to a modern bilingual children's book used in schools nationwide in states with high percentages of Spanish-speaking students. Originally it was written for New York City's School District Six, home to The Cloisters, the medieval museum of the Metropolitan Museum of Art.

Cosman, Madeleine Pelner. *The Medieval Baker's Daughter: La Hija de la Panadera Medieval.* Tenafly, 1984.

ON THE ALE-WIFE:
The Latin court case dates from the reign of King Edward III.

Letter Book G, Folio 137 (1364).

ON MARJORIE HORE:
The *fisshwyfe* punished on the thewe for endangering public health by selling stinking soles appears in a Latin document from the reign of King Edward III.

Letter Book G, Folio 292.

BEGGARS, GOSSIPS, AND SCOLDS

ON PUNISHMENT ON THE THEWE:

Alice Shether was punished for one hour as a common scold for molesting and annoying neighbors, inciting envy, defaming, backbiting, and sowing discord.

Letter Book H, Folio 21 (1375).

WITCHES

ON MEDICAL WOMEN AND WITCHCRAFT:

Beard, Mary. *Woman as a Force in History.* New York, 1946.

Cosman, Madeleine Pelner. "Criminalization of Women and Trials of Witches." A review of Helen Rodnite Lemay's *Women's Secrets, Pseudo-Albertus Magnus' De Secretum Mulieris. Journal of the History of Medicine and Allied Sciences,* March 1994.

———. "Regulating Childbirth in Medical Law History." A review of John M. Riddle's Contraception and Abortion from the Ancient World to the Renaissance. *Journal of the American Medical Association,* May 1995.

Forbes, Thomas. *The Midwife and the Witch.* New Haven, 1961.

Grillot de Givry, E. *Witchcraft, Magic, and Alchemy.* New York, 1971. Originally called *An Illustrated Anthology of Sorcery, Magic, and Alchemy.* Chicago, 1958.

Gross, C. "Modes of Trial in the Medieval Boroughs of England." *Harvard Law Review* 15 (1901): 695–701.

Kramer, H., and J. Sprenger. *Malleus Maleficarum.* 1487; *The Hammer of Witches.* Translated by M. Summers. London, 1928.

Lemay, Helen Rodnite. *Women's Secrets, Pseudo-Albertus Magnus' De Secretum Mulieris.* Albany, 1992.

Michelet, Jules. *Satanism and Witchcraft.* Translated by A. R. Allinson. New York, 1939.

Riddle, John. *Eve's Herbs: A History of Contraception and Abortion in the West.* Cambridge, 1997.

———. *Contraception and Abortion from the Ancient World to the Renaissance.* Cambridge, 1992.

Robbins, Rossell Hope. *The Encyclopedia of Witchcraft and Demonology.* New York, 1959.

Walker, Barbara. *The Woman's Encyclopedia of Myths and Secrets.* San Francisco, 1983.

ON DR. MARJORIE HALE:

Court Rolls of the Manor of Hales, 1270–1307, Worcestershire. Edited by John Amphlett and Sidney Graves Hamilton. London, 1912. Part 2: 403, 429, 449note, 550.

Talbot, C. H. and E. A. Hammond. *The Medical Practitioners in Medieval England: A Biographical Register.* London, 1965.

ON ACCUSATIONS OF NOBLE SORCERERS:

Professor Bellamy refers to allegations of sorcery against Duchess Eleanore Cobham of Gloucester; duchess of Bedford, Jacquetta of Luxemburg; and King Edward IV's mistress Jane Shaa.

Bellamy, John. *Crime and Public Order in England in the Later Middle Ages.* Toronto, 1973.

PHOTO CREDITS

1. From the *Da Costa Hours,* Bruges, 1520. Courtesy of The Pierpont Morgan Library, New York, Manuscript 399.
2. From the *Book of Hours of Catherine of Cleves,* Holland, 15th century. Courtesy of The Pierpont Morgan Library, New York.
3. From Ulrich von Richenthal's *Beschreibung des Constanzer Conziliums,* 1450–70, German. Courtesy of the New York Public Library, New York, Spencer Collection, Manuscript 32.
4. From Christine de Pizan, *Collected Works,* 15th century. Courtesy of The British Library, London, Harley Manuscript 4431.
5. From Albrecht Dürer, *Lovers,* late 15th century. Courtesy of the Metropolitan Museum of Art, New York.
6. From Christine de Pizan's *Othea,* 15th century. Courtesy of the Bodleian Library, Oxford University, Oxford.
7. From a 15th-century woodcut of *Four Sibyls.* Courtesy of Galeria Medievalia, San Diego, California.
8. From *Ars Moriendi,* Holland, 1465. Courtesy of Galeria Medievalia, San Diego, California.
9. From Ambrose Pare, *Oeuvres,* 1575. Courtesy of the National Library of Medicine, Bethesda, Maryland.
10. From Hans Weiditz, *Distillery,* Strassburg, Germany, about 1530. Courtesy of the Metropolitan Museum of Art, New York.
11. From *The Baths,* 14th century. Courtesy of Galeria Medievalia, San Diego, California.
12. From a *Book of Hours,* early 14th century, Flemish, Courtesy of Cambridge University, Trinity College Library, Cambridge, Trinity Manuscript B11.22.

13. From L. Thurneysser, *Quinta Essentia,* 1574. Courtesy of Galeria Medievalia, San Diego, California.
14. From Hans Burgkmair, *Der Weisskunig,* late 15th century. Courtesy of the Metropolitan Museum of Art, New York, gift of Anne and Carl Stein, 1961.
15. From a hand-colored woodcut, about 1470, South German. Courtesy of the Metropolitan Museum of Art, New York, Harris Brisbane Dick Fund, 1930.
16. From the *Manessischen Leiderhandschrift,* 14th century. Courtesy of the Bibliothek of the University of Heidelberg, Heidelberg, Germany.
17. From Hans Burgkmair, *Der Weisskunig,* late 15th century. Courtesy of the Metropolitan Museum of Art, New York, gift of Anne and Carl Stein, 1961.
18. From *Histoire de Renaud de Montauban,* France, 1468–1470. Courtesy of Bibliothèque de l'Arsenal, Paris, Manuscript 5073.
19. From M. Wohlgemuth, *Der Schatzbehalter,* A. Koberger, Nuremberg, 1491. Courtesy of the Metropolitan Museum of Art, New York, Rogers Fund, 1919.
20. From *Old Testament,* 13th century, French. Courtesy of The Pierpont Morgan Library, New York, Manuscript 638.
21. From Ulrich von Richenthal's *Beschreibung des Constanzer Conziliums,* 1450–70, German. Courtesy of the New York Public Library, New York, Spencer Collection, Manuscript 32.
22. From the *Da Costa Hours,* Bruges, 1520. Courtesy of The Pierpont Morgan Library, New York, Manuscript 399.
23. From the *Tacuinum Sanitatus,* 15th century, Italian. Courtesy of the New York Public Library, New York, Spencer Collection, Manuscript 65.
24. Iron and brass scale. 15th–16th centuries, Spanish. Courtesy of the Metropolitan Museum of Art, New York, Harris Brisbane Dick Fund, 1957.
25. From Johann Froschauer, *Kuchenmeisterei,* 1507, Ausburg, Germany. Courtesy of the Metropolitan Museum of Art, New York, Rogers Fund.
26. Courtesy of the Library of Alfred Rubens, Oxford and London.
27. From *Master of the Housebook,* late 15th century, German. Courtesy of Galeria Medievalia, San Diego, California.
28. From *Assiza Panis,* 14th century. Courtesy of the London Guildhall Library, London.
29. From Hans Baldung Green, *A Witches' Sabbath,* German, 1510. Courtesy of the Metropolitan Museum of Art, New York, Gift of Felix Warburg and Family, 1941.
30. From Geoffry de La Tour Landry's *Ritter von Turn,* Michael Furter, Basle, 1493. Courtesy of Galeria Medievalia, San Diego, California.

INDEX

Order of names: In general, names of medieval figures are alphabetized by given name followed by family name or place-name, as, for example, *Marie de France, Christine de Pizan.* Names of modern persons are alphabetized by family name first, as, for example *Twain, Mark.*

A

Aaron of Lincoln 100
abbess 47, 68–72, 127
abbey 52, 68, 71
Abelard, Pierre (Pierre) 70
abortion 127
abscess 31, 32
absolution 70, 111, 112
accomplice 115, 116, 119, 120
account books 20, 59–60, 102
adjudication of disputes 53, 69
adultery 5, 8, 36
adventurer 110
afeering 77
age of death 63
ages of man 49
Agatha, Maude's maid 116
agere et pati 27
Agnes, Medica 32
Agnes Moyses 116
agricultural tools 20, 22, 83, 87, 115
Albertus Magnus 125
alchemy 47
alderman 107
ale 60, 85, 87, 103, 104, 115, 117, 119–20
alembic 33, 47
alewife 87, 119–120
Alice de Beaufow 67
Alice de Caustone 119
Alice de Salasbury 121
Alice Garlic 119
Alice Grut 115
Alice Grym 115

Alice Knyvet 61
Alice Moyses 116
Alice Shether 121
Alice Wakefeud 120
allegory 15–17, 59
alma mater 71
alms 55, 85
alphabet invention 20
amulets 48
analgesics 32
Anastasia (artist) 20
anatomical studies 36
anatomists 29
Andreas Capellanus 4
anesthetics 32, 33
Anglo-Saxon 52
animal parts 33
annulment of marriage 52, 63
anti-aphrodisiac 48
Antidotarum (Nicholas of Salerno) 38
anti-feminism 1, 8, 18, 21
anti-Semitic denunciation 41, 106
anus 111–12, 126
aphrodisiac 33, 35, 48, 107, 108
apprentices 76, 79, 98, 99, 102, 107, 109, 110, 112
aquam clarissimam 39
Aquinas, Saint Thomas 47
Aquitaine 51
appearances 11
Aralais 6
arbitrator of disputes 53, 69
Aristotle 98, 125

arms and weapons xvii, 20, 61, 121
  arrow 28, 61
  bill 115
  bludgeon 115
  crossbow xvii
  glaive 61
  hatchet 115
  mummery 55
  sword xvii, 61, 115
  warfare treatise 15
Arthurian romance 7
Ars Moriendi 27
Art of Courtly Love 4
Art of Dying 27
assault 107, 124
asses's ears armor 121
Assize of Ale 87, 118
Assize of Bread 83, 89, 118
astrology 48, 49, 50, 52
astronaut 16–17
athenor 33
atour 65
authority 52, 55
autobiography 5–7, 15
autopsies 36
augury 48
Augustine, St. 123
aumbry 65, 85

B

backbiting 5, 121
backgammon 60
Baden-Baden 34
baker vii, xii, 75, 83, 88–9, 118–19